MW00883111

A Memoir

of

A Warrior of Love

for all of Humanity

by Phyllis K. Peterson

Other books by Phyllis Peterson

Assisting the Traumatized Soul

Healing the Wounded Soul

The Heroic Female Spirit

Remaining Faithful to Your Spouse

Seeking Intimacy in a Diverse Community:

Seeking the Spiritual Reality of the Mentally Ill

The Universal Theory of Man:

Authority of Self

The Skylark Life Skills Manual

for Women and Girls

The Sword of Truth:

A Sacred Fable

Princess Ruth and Samuel

The Magic that Happened

in the Pumpkin Patch

Northwest of the Butt

A Memoir of a Warrior of Love for Humanity

by

Phyllis Peterson

Skylark Publishing Company

© 2017 Phyllis K. Peterson

All quotations from the Baha'i Writings
used by Permission

Skylark Publishing Company
7945 Coopers Hawk Trail
Machesney Park, IL 61115
815-633-0492

www.skylarkpubl.com

DEDICATION

I dedicate this book to all the social workers, teachers, NGO's, doctors, psychologists, and psychiatrists who work in the field of education, prevention, and healing; and the children, youth, and adults that they serve. May they persevere in the face of burgeoning percentage rates of abuse, HIV/AIDS, human trafficking, rape, violation of trust, incest, and hopelessness; and know that their efforts have not been in vain.

ACKNOWLEDGMENTS

There are so many people I wish to acknowledge. During my journeys around the world, my ground crews have been amazing in their ability to organize my itinerary. They have "ploughed the field" decades before my arrival and established contacts with NGOs, schools, universities, principals, libraries, service organizations, and health organizations. They kept me safe from harm; they fed me, housed me, prayed with me. And while I was gone from my home community, my friends faithfully lifted me up in prayer. My husband, John, supported my mission wholeheartedly; though he missed me, he was willing to sacrifice for the people I wanted to serve. I thank the late Terry Cassiday, Ladan Cockshut, Mr. Nawarat and Mrs. Naiyana, Mojgan and Massoud Derkhshani, Dr. Kathryn Brown, Dr. Kathryn Moehling, Johnson Attah-Baaffour and his Ghanaian friend Koffi, Dale and Irma Allen, Dr. Marilyn Higgins, Naoko and Jun Kagami, Shiva Yan, Irene Taafaki, Agnes and Francis Reimers, Meena and Amin Sabet, Christiana Lawson, Dr. Beth Bowen who originally inspired and encouraged me to travel teach, and finally, my precious daughter, Nancy Good, who accompanied me to Swaziland, creates covers for many books, and gives great foot massages for my very tired feet.**TABLE OF CONTENTS**

Part Seven: Johannesburg and KwaZulu-Natal

p. 235

INTRODUCTION

People ask me, "What motivated you to become a Bahá'í and to travel teach so much?" I have reflected on this question frequently and always come back to six events in my past. First of all, I was influenced greatly by my Grandfather, Stephan Albano. Grandpa was from the old country, Palermo, Sicily in Italy.

He told me that in 1912 he received a vision in his late teens that God wanted him to convert from Catholicism to Protestantism. The family had been Catholic for generations. It must have caused him great consternation and foreboding to consider this. Indeed, when he told his parents of his intentions, they disowned him and he was forced to come to America to support himself. He left on a boat in November of 1912 determined to follow God on his new path. He had a brother in Rockford, Illinois and that was where he settled.

He met my Grandmother, Mamie Mazziotta Ferro, in Chicago and married her after she was widowed from her first husband, John Ferro, who was murdered by a Mafioso. This criminal was a member of the Black Hand group which practiced extortion. The Mafia man wanted Mamie to divorce Mr. Ferro and to marry him. She refused to do so, so he killed Mr. Ferro. If this incident had not occurred, my mother would never have been born, therefore I would never have been born and become a Baha'i. Was this the hand of God or the Black Hand? It's a haunting puzzle, but I believe it was an act of God.

My mother, Kathryn Albano Taylor, was born in Detroit, Michigan in 1920 on the day that was to become the Day of the Covenant. My Grandfather's conversion became the reason I was not raised as a Catholic. Some of my first memories at 3 years old are of my Grandfather preaching in Italian while I sat in a huge pew surrounded by my relatives. My Grandfather never became a minister but he was known to be very spiritual. I have vivid memories of him reciting over and over again the words "Hallelujah" and "Glory" while he was working in his garden, making dandelion wine, cobbling shoes and meditating. Much like Baha'is recite "'Allah'u'Abhá" during periods of meditation.

The second event was when I was 8 years old. My Baptist Sunday School teacher told the class that Chinese children were going to hell because they didn't believe in Jesus. I responded, "Would that be true if they haven't heard of Jesus?" She replied, "Yes!" Even at 8 years old I recognized that that was unjust, but I held my tongue. It was also the beginning of distrust of religious authority. Time would justify my outrage and disappointment.

I was 15 years old when the next event happened. I was reading an article in the Rockford Register Republic newspaper about a man who was traveling the world while visiting all the churches, temples, synagogues, and Holy places on his tour. I thought, What FREEDOM! How could he do this?

I wanted to do this! The Baptists had told me that all the people of other religions were going to hell. The next Sunday I decided to march myself down to the Court Street Methodist Church. I found out that they were good people who were worshiping God. The Sunday following that I went to the Presbyterian church and learned that they were wonderful people, too. I didn't know it at the time, but this was the beginning of my interest in the Interfaith movement. (That was 1957. In 2014 I became the President of the Rockford Interfaith Council.)

In 1964 my first husband was in the Air Force and was assigned to Naha Air Force Base on Okinawa. I was transferred there, too, with our three children. Every Sunday I attended church at the on base chapel and sang in the choir with Methodists, Lutherans, Nazarenes, Presbyterians, Episcopalians, Congregationalists and more, and my horizons were expanded. The Okinawan/Buddhist/Shinto people welcomed me as family. My mind and heart awakened like never before. I formed close friendships with people who previously were off limits to me. Everyone and everything was inclusive. I breathed for the first time the oneness that I was longing for.

But when I left the island of Okinawa and came home, all the churches I attended felt foreign to me in their exclusivity. I felt like I was betraying my friends on Okinawa, so I began searching. Judaism, Rosicrucianism, Theosophy, Unitarianism, and more. I couldn't find a home. Then, finally, a newspaper article about a Baha'i Fireside intrigued me. It was a night of a temperature inversion with fog surrounding this mysterious home and I paused at the door wondering, Is this just one more thing that's going to take me away from Jesus Christ?

I rang the doorbell, the door opened and I felt my breath hugged out of my lungs by Kathy Karlberg (now Kathy Roesch), former wife of Stig Karlberg. These two people became a strong influence on my life and my path. They gave me courage to independently investigate truth, which is one of the major principles of the Bahá'í Faith. Rockford became a "goal" city to create a community of Baha'is. All my questions were answered that pivotal evening and I found my home in the Bahá'í Faith. It wasn't taking me away from Christ; it was adding to my belief in Christianity through progressive revelation. This was in 1969.

I have written in my first book, "Assisting the Traumatized Soul," about my healing process during which I became inactive from 1972 through 1982. I became active again in 1983. I felt Bahá'u'lláh's guidance through those inactive years. And confirmation as I researched.

The fifth major experience I had happened because of the San Francisco Peace Conference in 1986. I had arranged to fly from Rockford to San Francisco with an elderly Bahá'í woman, who backed out at the last minute. I was terrified! I was going to have to travel alone. I took the bus from

Rockford to O'Hare and called my husband, John, sobbing to him that I couldn't do this. He said, "You don't have to. Just come home." "No, I don't want to," I cried. He comforted me on the phone the best way he could.

I got on the plane with tears rolling down my cheeks, wishing I didn't have to go alone. There was a layover in Salt Lake City where I called a friend in Rockford. She told me, "You don't have to go. Just turn around and come home." "No, I want to at least try." I cried in desperation at my fear. Next stop, San Francisco and my fear grew! I arrived at the hotel and immediately called my husband. Sobbing in my fear of being in this strange place. He comforted me and told me I could still come home. I told him I would think about it and if I couldn't "settle down and compose myself," I would come home. I said goodbye and hung up.

Just then a woman caught my eye. She had several pieces of luggage and an unmanageable number of bags that she was trying to load onto the elevator without success. I asked her if I could help. She looked grateful for the offer. Her name was Ruby and she was Native American. We got everything on the elevator and she took me to Kevin

Locke's room. What a blessing, I was serving and I forgot my fear. I called my husband and told him I was alright and had decided to stay. He was relieved.

I was thrilled to be at the Peace Conference! Carried away by the music! I met an elderly Baha'i woman named Eva Mae Davidduke who had met 'Abdu'l-Bahá in 1912 during his visit to America.

'Abdu'l-Bahá had told this story in her presence. She related it to me at dinner in a Chinese Restaurant at the closing of the conference. 'Abdu'l-Bahá said there was a group of people who were caravanning to another city. In the group there was a woman who was sick and crying that she couldn't go because she was too ill. 'Abdu'l-Bahá said that she didn't have to go, that he would make arrangements for her to stay and be taken care of in their absence. She replied that she wanted to try.

They travelled on to the next oasis and she begged for relief, she had to go back. 'Abdu'l-Bahá said he would make arrangements for her to be taken back in safety. She sobbed that she wanted to go on. They made their way to the next oasis, she on her donkey; and she sobbed again that she had to go back. She was too ill to go on. 'Abdu'l-

Bahá showed her the deepest sympathy and said they would take her back immediately and provide for her care. She replied that she wanted to go on to see if she could make it. This went on till they were half way there, and she began to feel better. She realized that it was the same distance back as it was to their destination. Finally they got to the end of their journey and she was well and happy.

Now, Eva Mae Davidduke did not know my story of travelling to San Francisco, but she was guided to tell me this story which gave me a sense of purpose. From then on I was no longer afraid to travel alone. Indeed, I have been to Thailand, Swaziland, Botswana twice, China twice, Japan twice, the Marshall Islands, and KwaZulu-Natal in South Africa to teach the Faith and my program "Protective Behaviors for Children." Teaching approximately 20,000 children and adults. Which except for my experience on the way to the San Francisco Peace Conference I couldn't have done.

And finally, the sixth thing that influenced me to become a travel teacher was reading "The Tablets of the Divine Plan" by 'Abdu'l-Bahá. It created such a longing within me to travel teach. In the late '80s early 90's I met Pioneer to

Japan, Dr. Marilyn Higgins who lives in Yamaguchi, Japan. We found that we had similar philosophies about moral authority and children. She invited me to come for a visit. My husband and I accepted and went to Japan in 2002. I met a woman in Tokyo by the name of Naoko Kagami. She learned about my program "Protective Behaviors for Children" and shared her childhood trauma with me and the group I was teaching. She eventually moved to Thailand with her husband and children.

When I returned home, Naoko e-mailed me, asking me to come to Thailand to teach my program and the Faith and that she would pay my way! I was in shock! How could I say no to such generosity of spirit? Of course, I said yes! But I didn't know that I was going to meet with resistance from two members of my family who tried to talk me out of my plans. "Something dreadful is going to happen to you." "John is going to leave you." "You're putting yourself in danger." "You're going to DIE!!!" This roused all my old fears, and doubts began to set in. Could I really do this? What if I got lost? I didn't speak the language, how would I find my way? Maybe they are right!

But then I thought of sweet Eva Mae Davidduke and her story about 'Abdu'l-Baha, and I became calm. Courage was instilled in me. I remembered my trip to the San Francisco Peace Conference and knew I could have the bravery necessary and the confirmations would come to me as they had before. Thus began my journey to Thailand in October of 2003. I now go to the report of my trip to the Office of Pioneering.

PART ONE

Thailand
October 8 through November 16, 2003

3:00 AM, October 8th: I am a mixture of excitement and apprehension which is interrupting my sleep. There are so many unknowns ahead of me. I have a sense of adventure as well as a desire for safety as I prepare my heart and mind for thirty-five days in Thailand. I am so wakeful trying to hold faith in my heart and the recognition that there is also the possibility of danger for anyone traveling alone in a foreign country, especially a woman.

I will be in Thailand during the APEC Conference (Asian Pacific Economic Cooperation) when 21 world leaders, including President Bush, will be in attendance. Security will be tight in Bangkok. The purpose of my journey is to teach "Protective Behaviors" to children, as well as to conduct training programs to the staff of schools and orphanages. I will also be presenting workshops on the topics of boundaries and the connection of spirituality to chastity at a three day Baha'i Youth Camp in which 35 youth will be participating. In addition I will be doing storytelling on the subject of the equality of women and men and presenting Firesides teaching about the Baha'i Faith and its Founder, Bahá'u'lláh.

John, my husband, who is also co-owner of the Bookstall of Rockford, a used book store, is wakeful, too. We say prayers together at this early hour. It is a calming and peaceful moment. I have a small, warm, comforting breakfast and then return to sleep for another three hours.

6:00 AM, October 8: I arise and finish last minute packing. I'm all business now and no longer have a conflicted mind and heart. When my heart is set on teaching, emotional conflict is usually resolved. All I have to do is jump in with two feet.

8:50 AM, October 8: John and I kiss goodbye at the bus terminal. He shows the most emotion he has shown in a long time. I pray that my husband of 24 years will understand why I want to go, especially for so long. He has always supported me in the past, but I know I am asking a lot of him this time. He tells me he's going to miss my cheerfulness and I respond that I will miss his calm, steady ways, as well as his humor that helps me laugh at myself when I am so serious.

I arrive at the United Airlines terminal at 10:20 AM and my luggage is checked in within 30 minutes. My plane departs at 12:50 PM for Narita Airport in Tokyo, Japan. Within 30 minutes of being in flight, I begin crying because I know I will miss John and I worry about my 83 year old mother, Kathryn. The week before my departure I prepared 15 days worth of meals for her and put them in the freezer in case she would have any type of emergency.

I arrive at Narita Airport at 3:30 PM on October 9th.

October 9: My next plane was to leave at 6:30 PM but it took off at 7:30 PM. I reset my watch to Bangkok time, which was 5:30 PM, 12 hours ahead of Rockford time. I arrived in Bangkok at 11:15 PM, 9, 161 miles from home. My trip has taken approximately 22 hours.

My first order of business is to report to Immigration and present my passport and visa. There are several lines to accommodate all of the passengers. I have prepared ahead of time by filling out a form prior to debarking the plane.

Their system works very smoothly and I am on my way to baggage in15 minutes. There were perhaps 12 people in line ahead of me.

I collected my baggage within 30 minutes and proceeded to Customs. This form I have also filled out on the plane. There was a box to check to declare even if you were unsure. I had brought medicine with me for over 40 days in case I would have a delay in returning. I declared it just to be sure I was within the regulations.

The Customs official asked me to show her my medicine. She asked me for a document from my doctor to show proof that I was authorized to have this medicine. Fortunately the last thing I had done before I left for O'Hare was to make a copy of the insurance company receipts for each of my medications. I showed that to her. She examined everything and said that it looked like a year's supply. I told her that I just wanted to be prepared for any eventuality. I whispered "Ya'Bahá'u'll'Abhá."

She was very businesslike and official about it all. And then left me standing there while she went to an office 25 feet away. She had not dismissed me. I stood there wondering and waiting for 10 to 15 minutes for her to return. Finally, a man appeared from another direction and I asked him if I was free to go. He didn't know so I sent him after the woman in the office. He returned and said, "Yes, you may go." Praise God!

I went out the exit door to attempt to find the person who was to meet me at the airport. I was in the wrong area. I was also apprehensive and exhausted from handling my suitcase and two carryon bags. So I sat down to rest and think. Should I wait till Sunantha Smith found me? Or should I go looking for her? I prayed for an answer. I looked up and saw a sign on a stand that said, "Meeting Place" with an arrow. I confidently followed the arrow and indeed saw many people who were holding up signs with names for those who were arriving, but none for me. Maybe she wasn't here yet? I said the Remover of Difficulties.

I thought, move to the public telephone area. A man was finishing a call while I was taking out paper money. He sensed my dilemma and offered a coin saying that he would dial a number for me. I gratefully accepted his offer. When I took out the contact information for my friend who was a member of the Spiritual Assembly of the Bahá'ís of Thailand, he noticed the word "Bahá'í" and told me there had just been an announcement for a Bahá'í over the public address system. He knew where my contact was waiting and told me where to go. I followed his direction and there was Sunantha Smith waiting for me with a sign that had my name on it. She greeted me with a big smile, took me to her truck and we were on our way to the Bahá'í Center!

I had been following the weather reports for Thailand on the internet for two or three weeks, so I was somewhat prepared for the heat and humidity. But when we left the airport to get into her truck, I realized that the real struggle and challenge would be in the mid-day sun, when it was usually 90 degrees plus with 95% humidity. I said my prayers of thanks and praise, grateful to crawl into bed at 1 AM with an air conditioner and fan to cool my room. God is good!

October 10th: I arose at 9 AM to a delightful ham and eggs breakfast with tea prepared by Sunantha. Another Bahá'í from Thailand had traveled by bus to go to the Bahá'í Youth Camp. His name was Na-Leen and he spoke some English so we were able to communicate.

After breakfast, at 10 AM, I signed onto the internet to e-mail my husband that I had arrived in safety and that I was in good hands. At 11:30 AM Sunantha and I were back in the truck on the way to the airport for the next leg of my journey. My plane, Thai Airways, was to leave at 12:55 PM. While standing in line to present my ticket, I observed a sign that stated

"Anyone caught bringing drugs into the country will receive the death penalty." So that is why I was asked so many questions about my medication. I was so glad I had declared to the customs official. I certainly hoped my medication wouldn't be considered "Drugs." Fortunately no one checked my carry-on bag from then on. But I had been up front to begin with so I felt safe. However, I was fearful that someone might steal my medication.

I had my first small Thai meal on the airplane and it was quite delicious!

The plane arrived at 2 PM at Obon International Airport. I collected my baggage and went out to those who were awaiting passengers. Mr. Nawarat and his wife, Mrs. Naiyana were holding up a sign with my name on it. They are the Principal and Administrator respectively of Santitham School in Yasothon in the northeast part of Thailand. The school serves 763 students - kindergarten and primary. The teachers' salaries are funded by the government and the parents take care of the cost of books and food. The school has received awards from the King for being the best private school in Thailand. Half of the students are children of government workers and those connected to the military, and the other half are children of business owners.

The school is a Bahá'í inspired school founded by Baha'is, and is allowed to teach a spiritual path to life through Bahá'í concepts as long as it meets the 70% required subject matter as determined by the government. The school is designed, however, to teach about all of the world religions and the principles of each.

Mr. Nawarat and Mrs. Naiyana and their two daughters. Nija, a 17 year old young woman who is autistic, and her 15 year old sister, Ninin, were my companions, guides, and teachers for the next two weeks. We drove the 90 kilometers in lively chatter to Yasothon where the school was located.

I asked about the King of Thailand and what kind of person he was. Mr. Nawarat said he was highly respected because he was very compassionate toward the poor. His name is King Bhumipol Adulyadej, which means Lord of the Land. Queen Sirikit is beloved, too, because she is dedicated to enhancing the lives and opportunities of the people. Her name means "glorified," referring to her beauty and goodness. She is greatly admired because of the many projects she has in every province of Thailand. Her projects include avenues of profit for artists and crafts people. She has introduced Thai arts in all the major cities of the world (including Paris, London, and New York) so that her people will have respected professions.

The drive takes about one hour and 15 minutes. Mr. Nawarat takes me to my hostess' home to drop off my luggage and to meet her. Baby is her name. But do not be fooled by this name. She is a highly gifted and qualified physics teacher, who is adept at scaling down the concepts for primary age students. I am soon to find out that these very gentle people, who have multi-syllable names that I couldn't possibly remember, also have Americanized nicknames, such as Khun FM, Khun Meow, Khun Eyes, and Khun Dame; Khun being a term of respect applying to either male or female.

Mr. Nawarat and Mrs. Naiyana took me out to dinner to celebrate my first day in Yasothon. She ordered a traditional Lemon Grass soup plus other dishes that were unknown to me. The soup was quite honestly the best soup I've ever had in my life. However, though Mrs. Naiyana asked the chef NOT to put a lot of chilies in the dishes, the soup in particular was eating a hole in my stomach. I was warned that cooks will have their way in Thailand and if asked to tone down the chilies and the MSG, they may put in twice as much.

I was also warned by the guide book for Thailand that I found in my local library that I should drink only bottled water in which the seal had not been broken. Once my stomach settled down, (within an hour) I was more comfortable and knew that with guidance I could make myself into a good traveler and guest.

We returned to Khun Baby's home to the sound of fireworks in every street we drove down. This was the end of the Buddhist Lenten season. The moon was full and it was time for the people to celebrate. As we approached Baby's house, someone was lighting candles all over the gate and the fence that surrounded it. It was Baby's father; he greeted me with great honor even to the point of untying my shoes and personally removing them, telling me that his house was now my house, too. A perfect example of how gracious the people of Thailand are to their guests.

The challenge of the heat and humidity and exhaustion from the time change finally forced me to shower and turn in for the night. I said my prayers and went to bed at 9 PM (9 AM our time) to the sound of fireworks; because homes are so close together and close to the streets, the sound thundered. Even this I was delighted with. I just smiled because it was the most unique way I had ever celebrated my birthday.

October 11: Today was my first day to explore the grounds of Santitham School. It is a complex of 8 buildings, some very modern, plus some open air shelter/classroom type of structures, and an open canteen/cafeteria area that has both exhaust fans and ceiling fans.

Gardens, tropical plants, trees and fish ponds are everywhere. Landscaped courtyards, fragrant flowers such as orchids and flowering trees and bushes abound. It is truly a paradise. The colors that surround me are purples and reds, pinks and orange.

Animals roam the grounds very slowly because of the heat. The heat even grinds sports to a halt for the energetic youth. One of the first things I noticed was the size of two different species of butterfly. One with a five inch span, the other with a six inch span. They dwarfed anything I had ever seen and they looked like the sparkling jewels of Thailand taking flight. The birds, too, were lovely, colorful and unusual with such sweet calls.

I met FM (16 years old) and Arm who want to go to the US and become movie directors, and Yui who wants to be a writer and who doesn't like the music of Thailand because it's about love, whereas the music of America is about life.

The first workshop was an exercise in chanting and singing. The youth committee that organized the camp activities presented them in an engaging and humorous way that kept the attention of those participating. Dinner was served at 6

PM followed by the step dancers from Canada, a group of youth who were travel teaching in Thailand. They were demonstrating skits and dances that were to be turned into workshops for the camp participants the following day. They were excellent dancers and dramatists. From Canada, Belgium and Australia, they are doing what is called "a year of service." They all have amazing energy, capacity, and knowledge of the Faith; and they have a sincere desire to serve mankind.

October 12: Today from 9 AM to 12 PM I presented my program "The Spiritual Challenge: Boundaries and Chastity," which offers that one cannot develop true unity and cooperation with others or obedience to authority unless their identity and boundaries are also protected. During this 3 hour program we played the Boundary Sculpting Game which I originally created for Family Violence Shelters and is now being used all over the United States. The game illustrates that we are all boundary violators and we have all had our boundaries violated. It also creates understanding of what we do unconsciously instead of consciously setting boundaries, how to acknowledge the feelings and needs of others, as well as the fact that it has to be reciprocal. The game is interactive and the youth seemed to grasp the concepts even though I had to express them through a translator. The model we acted out was an unwanted hug from a stranger, friend, coworker or relative, which was a paradox in this culture in which children seem to be high-touch while the parents usually hug behind closed doors. The youth seemed to want to explore this concept in great depth.

This was the day that the heat and humidity were so high that I felt like I was in the middle of a giant watermelon, baking in a hot Texas field in the middle of August. The youth could tell that I was overheated and were graciously bringing me water so I could cool down.

My program was followed by lunch; then the afternoon session offered the participants the opportunity to divide into groups for drama dance, following the tutelage of those who had presented the entertainment for us the evening before. At 4 PM there was a sports break. At 6 PM dinner. In the evening hour the youth who participated in the afternoon workshops demonstrated the dancing and drama they had learned from the Canadian youth. We also had a fabulous demonstration of a Thai Boxing Dance ritual expertly executed by Na-Lean. This dance is done before a boxing match to show respect for the boxer's teacher.

Each evening I would return to Khun Baby's home for a shower and to wash my clothes. She took such good care of me as if I was her mother. She fixed a wonderful breakfast for me every morning. She even did my laundry for me one day. She grabbed the basket from me, insisting it would make her happy to do it.

October 13: Today was the final day of the Camp. We started, as usual, with prayers and then they asked me to do some storytelling. I told stories I had written about the equality of women and men in which both had to overcome traditional roles in order for women to attain their highest possibilities and for men to attain the greatness that might be theirs. This is a Bahá'í principle that was taught by 'Abdu'l-Bahá, the Son of Bahá'u'lláh. I also told stories about the power of prayer. This was followed by exercises for various groups. We then closed the Camp with a short program that demonstrated what we had learned in the past three days. And thanks were given to God.

A delicious lunch was served with a real treat: coconut milk ice cream, which I tried my best to refuse but the youth insisted that it would cool my body and they would not take "no" for an answer. So, after 20 minutes of their begging, I capitulated to their urgent pleas. It is now my favorite ice cream.

At 4 PM the heat was so bad that I asked to be taken to Baby's house so that I could take a shower. The plan was dinner at 6:30 PM, shopping in the market till 7:45 PM, with a movie at the Cinema at 8 PM. By 10 PM I was back home and ready for another shower, even though the air-conditioned theatre provided some relief from the heat.

Khun Baby was a little late in picking me up for dinner that night. While I waited I sat in the small court yard in the front of her home, which was filled with lovely roses and tropical plants, including two towering coconut trees. I sat and watched two men next door chopping the husks off of their coconuts, cracking them open and pouring the milk into a vat. As I sat there in the twilight, I counted 23 lizards, harmless, surrounding me and could hear them chattering intermittently to one another. I could only imagine how many lizards must have been playing in the coconut trees.

Inside the house more lizards were frolicking on the walls and ceiling while Pierce Brosnan, playing James Bond was speaking Thai on TV. The commercials for the movie were about the upcoming APEC Conference. There were banners announcing the event every 20 feet at the Bangkok Airport when I arrived. Bangkok was preparing for any eventuality and security would be tight.

The movie was a delight! "Fan Chan" is about a boy growing up in Thailand whose only friend until he was 12 years old was a girl his age. He wants to fit in with the boys but they are bullies. Finally, he turns against his best friend who is heartbroken when he bullies her (at which point I gasp and cry). He becomes sensitive to what he has lost but it is too late because she moves away. He follows the family's truck down the highway trying to apologize and your heart follows with him, but he can never catch up. The final scenes of the movie are of him as a 28 year old adult man, receiving an invitation to her wedding. He arrives at the reception. She is there in her gown and veil with her back to him. I am dying to see what she looks like. She turns around, and there she is, the 12 year old girl in braids, radiantly smiling at him. I'm hoping to get a DVD of this movie in the future. (I did!)

October 14: Today I had to pack my bags to leave Baby's house. I was brought to Santitham School where I just hung out all day. I wrote14 pages in this journal to keep myself busy because most of the English speaking people were either very occupied or they had left. During the breaks I took from writing, I attempted to communicate with a few individuals I had not met previously.

It was a few degrees cooler today with a strong wind, which I had not experienced since I arrived in Yasothon. Then at 3:30 PM there came a sudden downpour, the first rain in the daytime I had seen. When the clouds broke open and the sun came out, the heat and humidity were stifling. One hour later, the sun was lower and the wind came up, driving some of the humidity out. I am looking forward to my next shower.

An Australian youth was taking a trip to Chiang Mai for the four day weekend, so my bags and belongings were moved into the dormitory that he vacated temporarily. The last thing he told me was that he found a poisonous snake in his room 3 months before I arrived. They come up from the river that borders the school. We are supposed to just wave them off because they are just as afraid of us as we are of them, except for the King Cobras. For my protection Mrs. Naiyana asked the maintenance staff to cut down and whack back all the weeds in the back of the dormitory. This is needful because I have to wash my clothes then hang them to dry in the back yard. I do not linger there; I am cautious and very fast. I also have to take long leaps over trails of large red ants that sting without provocation. There is a 24/7 trail one half inch over and around the doorway of my dormitory. It keeps me on edge, along with the snakes and mosquitoes, which carry dengue fever, a disease that attacks the blood cells and can cause death.

October 15: Today is a down day. I have an intestinal upset, headache and nausea all day. Part of it I believe is because I didn't drink coffee this morning and I had too much fresh pineapple the night before. I tried to prepare for my program tomorrow but felt the need to rest. Then Mr. Nawarat informed me that my all day training program for the teachers would be held on Friday, the 17th. That certainly brightened my day.

There was a worship service later in the evening, the Feast of Ilm or Knowledge. It was an intimate gathering in which all those present participated. I double-checked with Mr. Nawarat to make sure my training program was still on Friday, because I've noticed that things change quickly and sometimes I'm not informed till the last minute. He assured me that we were on for Friday.

October 16: I was sick all through the night. I awoke grateful that I would have another day to study and prepare. Immediately there came a knock on the door informing me that my training program started in 30 minutes! There was time only to get dressed and fix a slice of bread and peanut butter for breakfast. Everyone was waiting for me! I got over my embarrassment and proceeded with my all day workshop titled "Child Abuse Prevention: Protective Behaviors for Children" for 35 teachers. They were heartsick to hear the statistics on child abuse from countries around the world. One caring teacher thought that she was completely free from this problem because she didn't experience it in her childhood, but now realizes that the problem surrounded all of them.

There were many sad stories that they related, not unlike the stories that I have personally heard or read about in the U.S., England, South Africa, India, Brazil, or Eastern Europe to mention just a few places I have researched.

For example: South Africa has some of the highest incidences of child and infant rape in the world. In 2001, it was reported by the South African Police Service that children are the victims of **41 percent** of all rapes reported in the country. About **15%** of rapes are children under the age of 11 according to the MRC's Rachel Jewkes. India ranks among the top five countries with the highest rate of child sexual abuse. A 2013 report 'India's Hell Holes: Child Sexual Assault in Juvenile Justice Homes' by the Asian Centre for Human Rights explained the epidemic proportions of this problem, with over 48,000 child rape cases recorded between 2001 to 2011. There was a 336% increase in child rape cases during this time period. Despite these numbers, India has largely ignored the issue due to its taboo nature. In the United States 9.3% of cases of maltreatment of **children** in 2012 were classified as **sexual abuse**. 62,939 cases of **child sexual abuse** were reported in 2012. According to the Bureau of Justice **Statistics'** National Criminal Victimization Survey, in 2012, there were 346,830 reported rapes or **sexual** assaults of persons 12 years or older.[1]

These figures are shocking and when you put them against the statistics for HIV/AIDS (42%) which many perpetrators believe can be cured by having sex with a virgin child, they become even more shocking.

The exercises I prepared for my class were a source of great humor combined with embarrassment, creating ripples of laughter as we explored the concepts of how to teach children to protect private areas of their bodies and that they have a right to protect themselves. The Thai people as a culture are very shy and parents don't usually hug one another unless behind closed doors. But their laughter was also so enthusiastic and contagious that it helped to break through their shyness.

Their openness and honesty was refreshing and carried us through the workshop to a conclusion of questions and answers, with several of the teachers relating what they had learned from the training session. One woman felt brave enough to ask a very serious question. At a community

---

[1] Google and Wikipedia

event she found that a 4 year old boy had forced her 3 year old granddaughter into an oral sex position. She removed her granddaughter from the scene, but she didn't know what to do about the situation, how to address it. The boy's father was on the Local Spiritual Assembly with her and she didn't want to create disunity.

I told her that it wasn't an individual problem. It was a community problem and if she looked at it from that perspective she could find a solution. She had been trained in my program and now she had an opportunity to put her skills to work by organizing a "Protective Behaviors for Children" program in her community. She didn't have to point a finger at anyone in particular. Just begin the work of creating awareness and knowledge in the community. Because an aware child and parent means that the child has more protection than an unaware child.

Of course, it is an individual problem, too, but when you realize that the community has to rise up against it and you are part of that community, JUSTICE becomes your concern, too.

I am still sick but this late this afternoon is my time to do my laundry. I have two large, wide buckets, one with soapy water, the other with rinse water and I must scrub my clothes while on my hands and knees. Then I have to pick up the heavy bucket of dirty water and empty it into the shower stall and refill the bucket for the next sorted load. As I said earlier my dormitory is located next to the river. I have to carry the bucket of wet clean clothes to the back yard and hang them up. I bravely pretend I am Indiana Jones' grandmother, shake off my fear, deciding I'll wave a sock if approached by a snake.

Baby brought me dinner, a dish with rice noodles, and one of my favorites. She's a wonderful friend. My abdomen continues to rumble through the night. I finally drop off to sleep around midnight.

October 17: Today is cleaning day as the school is in preparation for Monday, the first day of school after the break. everyone is busy at their tasks; mothers are arriving at the office to register and pay for their children's books and meals. receipts are made out and everywhere you turn there is organization. Someone fixed a cup of Jasmine tea for me; I am enjoying it as I write in my journal. this particular tea comes from northern Thailand, the Chiang Mai area, which I hope to visit. but for now it is time for me to brace up my courage again and wander down to the dormitory to fetch my laundry from the back yard. I do it on the run!

I had a wonderful lunch of fried whole fish and fried chicken today. a steamed vegetable that tasted like a cross between asparagus and broccoli, plus a dish of slivered papaya with vegetables and chilies that accompanied it. Apparently Mrs. Naiyana has some difficulty with the very hottest of Thai foods because she kept panting while she ate the papaya dish but kept eating it anyway. Breathless, she urged me to try it, but Mr. Nawarat warned me against it. I wisely refrained!

Because Mrs. Naiyana had to go to the University 100 kilometers away, she asked me to accompany Mr. Nawarat this evening to the opening of the new Chinese Buddhist Temple in Yasothon. It is by invitation only and I will be allowed to take my camera. I brought a special dress for a special occasion, so this will be my opportunity to wear it.

This festive occasion requires that the streets are barricaded and the police keep things under control. We were served a 15

course Thai dinner with the Influence of Chinese, Laotian, Vietnamese and Malaysian cooking. the food just kept coming, most of which I did not know how to eat. I watched others to see how they were manipulating their chopsticks and using their one bowl, but felt terribly inept, while they effortlessly knew where to put their sauces and their shrimp tails. I was horrified that they disposed of them on the beautiful table cloth! By the end of the evening , I had accumulated four bowls to their one. Mr. Nawarat smiled at me knowingly. Also, while there was bottled water, there were also ice cubes. I didn't know if they were safe, so I just drank the water.

Finally, I was distracted by the evening's program. the Governor of Yasothon was invited to cut the ribbon to the Temple. He was surrounded by the Senators and those who had contributed several million Thai Baht for the building of the Temple that was to be used by the community. Following the official ceremony there was a performance of classical Thai dance by a young woman who was very skilled. I was told she performed a very difficult dance of a caliber that is often requested by the King of Thailand.

Various entertainers also graced the stage, but then the fun started.... homespun entertainment... as one after another the people began performing to karaoke. The chairman of the Chinese Association also sang. He is perhaps 70 years old. About six women pretended to be his adoring fans, rushing the stage with a single rose each, reaching for him. We all laughed at this moment of fun. I am so glad I had this opportunity, but I am also thankful that we left before dessert was served.

October 18: This morning I have accidentally locked myself out of my bedroom. I have a key to the front door of the dormitory, a key to the padlock on the screen door and a key to the room in which I keep my luggage and personal things, but the only time I lock the door to my bedroom is at night when I go to sleep. And when I contacted Mr. Nawarat to see if he had an extra key in the office, it was the worst possible timing for him. He was already helping two people. At least I have a shelter in the office in which to wait out of the heat.

I am supposed to go to the market this morning with Baby and Sogn but they haven't arrived yet. (Sogn admires the two Baha'i rings I am wearing and wants to know where she can purchase one. When I return to the U.S., I decide to send her my prettiest one.) So I have spent the morning researching the Writings of Baha'u'llah and in prayer. When I was most concerned about locking myself out of the bedroom, four sparrows perched on my window sill as if to remind me that, "His eye is on the sparrow and I know He watches me." It was comforting.

In three hours many people came with different sets of keys and could not find a match. Finally, they called a locksmith to open the door. Two allen wrenches and it was done. I was assured of a good night's sleep on a firm mattress with a fan.

At 4 PM I tried to take a shower but the water was off; so I put on clean clothes to attend the devotional meeting at Golee's house. The youth of Yasothon were present, many of whom had attended the camp. We started at 5 PM by learning a song, with devotions 30 minutes later. We sat and chatted after prayers and I received a treat from home. Oreo cookies! By the time I returned to the dormitory, the water was back on and I had a blessed, cooling shower.

October 19:   All over the world Bahá'ís are commemorating the Birth of the Bab this evening. Golee's air-conditioned truck sped through people filled streets that were bustling with everything from motorbikes and cars to rickshaws, then we carefully made our way over bumpy roads and through a rice paddy to the home of a lovely Bahá'í couple who were hosting the celebration.

I had the joy of watching the sun set over the rice paddy, while listening to Dash Croft on a CD singing, "Look at me, follow me, be as I am, 'Abdu'l-Bahá, 'Abdu'l-Bahá!" Every celebration in Thailand is held outdoors. The entire front yard of this home, enclosed by a five foot wall with a gate, was concrete, perhaps 30 by 30 feet. With the exception of a six foot square area that was landscaped, grassy, with a tree in its center. Lights were hung from the house to poles. Grass mats were in the middle of the courtyard where all the guests were to sit cross-legged.

Anecdotes of the Bab's life were read as well as prayers, followed by singing. I was surrounded by youth who were singing songs in Thai that were familiar to me. I felt at home. Many of the youth were new Bahá'ís filled with enthusiasm for the Faith and love for Bahá'u'lláh.

October 20: I awoke early in order to attend the opening of "Back to School." The students of Santitham School raised the Thai flag, said prayers for the Holy day and gave honor through song to the King of Thailand. The entire group of 763 students stood outside in the sunshine, amidst the many shades of green trees and plants and sang: "Say: God sufficeth all things above all things!" A brief history of the Bab and His life was offered. It was a thrill and indeed overwhelming to see the vision of Bahá'u'lláh fulfilled at this school which should be a blueprint for every Baha'i community in the U.S.

After the opening ceremony, children were dismissed to their classes and each individual teacher then took up the task and further teaching the story of the Bab in detail from Ruhi Book Three...the entire school! As I write this they are singing, "We are drops of one ocean," and the teacher is writing the word "unity" on the blackboard.

These were some of the behaviors, emotions, and expressions I witnessed in the 4th grade primary class I sat in on: Squirmy, boisterous, shy, giving, impish, clever, quick to memorize, confident, inquiring, cool, laid back, indignant, joy, helpfulness, friendliness, dramatic, teasing, anger, artistic, laughter, and bullying.

Mrs. Naiyana walked me to my dormitory this evening in the dark. When I unlocked all of my locks, a giant cricket came inside. She told me it was a cockroach. I said, "I beg your pardon, I know a cricket when I see one and I want desperately to believe this is a giant cricket instead of a cockroach." She took off her shoe and killed it and that was that.

October 21: Naoko Kagami, whom I originally became acquainted with when I was travel teaching in Japan, arrived at 11 AM with her four children after a 10 hour ride from her city, Banchang in Rayong. I had forgotten how fast things move when you have four children. I am now unable to keep up with my journal, not only because of the children, but because I now have someone to speak with in English. I can accomplish a lot of writing when I am lonely.

We stayed at a hotel this evening, and to my dismay, I discovered that I could not lock the sliding door to my balcony, 3rd floor. Since I didn't know if it was safe to take a shower, I turned on the air conditioner and cooled down while I said many prayers for protection. I do not speak Thai so I could not call the desk and ask for help. Naoko had already retired for the night with the baby and the three older children; I could not disturb them. I decided that I had to trust in God. The next day Khun Jam Long found out about my unlocked door from Naoko and insisted that my room be changed so that I could sleep in safety. Fortunately and wisely, I always carried my valuables with me wherever I went so at least I felt like I was acting in a self-protective way.

October 22: A day that is lost to memory!

October 23: Mrs. Naiyana and Mr. Nawarat took us out to dinner at a 5 star hotel restaurant where we ate fish teriyaki and lemon grass soup among other traditional Thai dishes. I discovered that the Thai cooks do not remove shrimp heads when they cook the soup, but they are easily removed and discarded because they are tender from cooking.

October 24: Today Mrs. Naiyana received her Master's Degree after a long, involved and frustrating process that would have discouraged a saint. We waited at her home for her return from the University, where we were allowed to shower, all six of us, before our return trip to Bangkok. Always thinking ahead, Mrs. Naiyana had asked a dear Baha'i friend to serve her guests in her absence. Our supper was sticky rice, omelets and chicken teriyaki.

After her return, we celebrated her accomplishment and at 9 PM Naoko, her four children and I loaded into the 12 passenger Toyota van for the 8 hour trip to Bangkok. Mr. Nawarat had an appointment with the Spiritual Assembly of Thailand so he rode with us as well, with Khun Jam Long driving.

October 25: We arrived in Bangkok at the Nonthaburi Bahá'í Center at 5:30 AM. By the time we went upstairs, the children were wide awake. Fortunately, I was able to go to a separate room and rest until 10 AM. I met Sammi, a woman who is pioneering in the south of Thailand. She is a well-travelled, capable woman who never stops serving the Cause of God, nor does her 70 year old husband.

We had lunch that was cooked in a small restaurant down stairs from the center. After lunch we walked to a Bahá'í run kindergarten that was owned by Khanum, an Indian woman who is extremely well educated in child development. It was after hours and we were not able to enter the school. We attempted to walk to her condominium and tried to phone her to no avail, so I asked to walk straight to the Center as I was extremely over-heated. Naoko said my face was very red.

We returned to the Center. I drank a lot of water and took a shower to cool down, then I lay down to rest and stabilize my system. Thankfully, I felt better in two hours. This night Naoko and the children joined me in my room so that the men could sleep in the other room. At 10 PM Jun, Naoko's husband, arrived. He greeted everyone and the children were delighted to see him. They were disappointed that they couldn't spend more than a few moments with him before he went to the men's quarters. They hadn't seen him in over 5 days. Soon sleep took over their disappointment and they were resting well.

October 26: Today is an important day for me. We are to go to the Bangkok Baha'i Center to wait until the Spiritual Assembly meeting is over, as Mr. Nasser and Mrs. Maliheh will drive me to Chiang Mai, in the northwest of Thailand.

While we are waiting, I have the opportunity to meet many of the Bahá'í friends, all with bright, cheerful faces, warm smiles and filled with love for Baha'u'llah. Mr. Nasser is also on the Spiritual Assembly of Thailand and his wife, Mrs. Maliheh is an Auxiliary Board Member. It is a 7 hour trip to Chiang Mai, a city that I had heard so much about and longed to visit. We pulled in at midnight. Quite oddly, my husband, the co-owner of the Bookstall of Rockford, had just that month sent a book to one of his customers in Chiang Mai. I was hoping to meet him. We had corresponded by e-mail to try to set things up.

October 27: I was soon to learn that my hosts were fruitarians. Mr. Nasser had been ill a few years earlier and was guided to learn about the healing qualities of fruit. I didn't know if I could exist on a steady diet of only fruit for one week, but I was willing to give it a try. I learned what fruits can be combined and those which cannot. I learned that watermelon must be eaten alone. All of the fruits were fresh and were purchased daily from the open-air fruit market. I must say that I felt that every cell of my body was rejuvenated by this diet. But I missed my protein.

At 9 AM we went to Mr. Nasser's business which is called Shiraz Jewelry. He had a vast collection of jewels that were typical of Thailand, but most interesting of all, the store seemed to be a meeting place for visiting Bahá'ís from Iran, Malaysia, Great Britain, Canada, Australia, Germany, Spain, and of course, I was visiting from America.

Everyone had exciting stories to relate and when Mr. Nasser heard my snake story from the dormitory, he told me he was standing outside that very building when a green snake approached him. As he had caught many snakes while growing up as a young boy, he reached out for the snake to catch it. The snake reared up its head in a springing motion and started spitting at him! It was a King Cobra! The cobra tries to spit its venom into your eyes, but as he was a tall man, the venom hit him in his upper chest and his arms. Wherever the venom struck it was icy cold and fiery hot at the same time. He killed the snake with a big stick and then went to wash himself.

Hearing this story inspired Mrs. Maliheh to tell the story of the two snakes who were doing a love-mating dance in the back office of Shiraz Jewelry one afternoon. She thought it was charming and romantic but Mr. Nasser wanted to kill the snakes. She countered with calling the zoo and having them captured. They attempted to do the humanitarian thing but the zoo said they did not offer such services. The police also turned them down. By this time the snakes went out of the office and under the building. Mrs. Maliheh wanted to allow them the freedom to go their way. However, Mr. Nasser countered with the fact that he did not want 30 to 40 baby snakes under the building. So, somehow he got the snakes out from under the building. One of his staff took the huge bag of snake home and made a wonderful pot of snake soup. Whether this is a happy or sad ending depends on if you are the cook or the snake!

October 28: This is the day I went exploring on my own after a confidence building talk with Mr. Nasser. I wanted to go up to the Buddhist temple and take some photographs. The temple was perhaps 1 1/2 blocks from Shiraz Jewelry. I set off with my money bag and my passport under my dress, purse with a few Baht around my neck and my camera. Walking along the street I saw more foreign people than Thai people. Chiang Mai is a very popular city in Thailand, the second largest, so it draws a lot of tourists. As I walked inside the gate of the temple, a woman with a tray of captured birds came up to me. She indicated that if I purchased one of these birds and set it free, I would have good luck for the rest of my life. One of my hopes in coming to Chiang Mai was to purchase gifts for my children, grandchildren and husband. I decided against buying a bird, politely declining.

Outside of the temple was a tall standing Buddha, magnificent in peaceful countenance and ornamentation. Standing at the bottom of the stairway I saw that the railing leading up was actually several long dragons, the head and body of each coming out of the mouth of another, presumably there to protect the temple and the Buddha within. Circling the outside of the temple were white statues of slender spiritual beings that foretold of the spiritual experience awaiting those who ventured up the stairs. I slowly walked up the stairs, my hand gliding over the scales of the dragons and respectfully took off my shoes before I entered the temple.

Inside were three beautifully constructed statues of the Buddha. One of them is said to be the largest teakwood carved Buddha in Asia. Another looked as though it was made from a giant emerald jewel, but that would have been impossible. There were flowers in front of each Buddha and the whole setting instilled peace in ones' soul. I decided to sit down and say a prayer of thanks to God. I sat there thinking of my own spiritual journey that had taken me from the fundamentalist Baptist church as a child, to the Nazarene church which believed in sanctification, to sitting in a choir on Okinawa with people of many Christian denominations, to the Unitarian Universalist church, to the Lutheran church, and now the Bahá'í Faith, and I feel content and privileged. I thought of my friends who are members of the Interfaith Council of Rockford, Illinois and realized how all of these experiences had changed my life. Needless to say, I left the Buddhist temple reluctantly.

I walked down the street, past Shiraz Jewelry and explored several gift shops. It was quite the contrast after the temple and decided rather than break the spell of my experience, ducked into a tea shop that I had heard about. A woman who had her own tea plantation owned it. She actually grew the tea that she served in her gift shop/restaurant. I ordered some Jasmine green tea and relaxed while looking at the large murals of her tea plantation. What a relief to be out of the heat and humidity for a while.

Before I left I added to my teapot collection, purchasing a small green elephant teapot that was made in Chiang Mai. I had been gone perhaps an hour and a half and decided to check in with Mr. Nasser. I walked in the door and the first thing he said was, "You survived!" Not only did I survive, I didn't buy the bird. Mr. Nasser told he thinks the birds are trained and once released, they go back to the woman's home waiting to be fed the birdseed with which she captures them to begin the process all over again.

October 29: I was lucky enough to have lunch with an English woman in a small Thai open-air cafe on this day. She suggested items on the menu that she had enjoyed in the past and I was very pleased with the items. People ask me what I ate while I was in Thailand and for the most part, I do not know or cannot name it because I don't speak Thai. I had such a wide variety of offerings. My friend ordered a soup that was extremely hot, so hot that she could not eat it. She asked the chef if she had some yogurt that she could stir into the soup. The chef immediately went down the road to a store to purchase the yogurt for the soup. This is not because the restaurant seeks to be competitive, but rather because the Thai people have a genuine desire to serve and please.

I had to cut my luncheon short because I was scheduled to have a private consultation with a young woman back at the jewelry store. During my stay in Thailand I was called upon to use every bit of knowledge I had learned. People were seeking knowledge of everything from how to overcome trauma of childhood abuse, domestic violence, marriage problems, ostracism, to how to regulate their anger. It is my sincere hope that I gave encouragement that was consistent with the Writings of Bahá'u'lláh. Mr. Nasser said that the next time he saw this particular woman, she was walking tall with head upright and shoulders back. I was filled with gratitude to God.

Another program on "Protective Behaviors for Children" had been planned for the evening. Thankfully, it started with a meal that included chicken! Real protein! I hadn't had protein in 4 days. I tried to eat as though I wasn't starving.

The people who attended this program were hungry for knowledge on how to prevent child abuse. The statistics on child sexual slavery in Thailand are 250,000 to 300,000. Another English woman was in Thailand because she feared that her two grandchildren were going to be sold into slavery. Her son had married a Thai woman and they later divorced. The son never received Thai citizenship papers because, as he was in the Navy, he didn't think it necessary. And the children were considered Thai rather than British even though the mother had given them up. It was a very confusing situation to try to negotiate, and heartbreaking to see the anguish and helplessness this woman was feeling.

October 30: I could never have successfully shopped by myself in Chiang Mai. Two days prior to this I stopped into a shop and couldn't properly bargain to purchase an inexpensive necklace. So, tonight Maliheh took me shopping in the night bazaar. Tiny tents and homemade structures were wall to tall, curb to curb, facing more permanent stores as we walked down the street. Vendors were hawking everything from T-shirts and china to opera glasses, Thai costumes and table runners.

I watched in amazement as Maliheh bargained for T-shirts for my grandchildren. The quality of these shirts was beautiful and I would have paid full price for them but Maliheh said they were always priced higher for the unwary tourist. If she didn't get the price she thought fair, we just walked on to another vendor.

The week before I came to Thailand, my husband and I saw the opera, "Lucia de Lammermoor" at the Coronado Theatre. He brought his usual small telescope, which provided a closer view but definitely was not elegant. A vendor was selling opera glasses and binoculars so I took time to look through the selection. The price started at 1600 Baht and Maliheh said "No!" We could do better.

He kept lowering the price and finally told us the lowest price he would take. Maliheh urged me down the street. I told her I wanted to try one more time. We went back and I made an offer lower than his lowest and because he was so glad to see us come back, he took it! Happy Birthday, John. (The vendor probably still made a lot of money!)

October 31: I was supposed to fly back to Bangkok early this morning, but my schedule was preempted for another private consultation. I spent the morning and early afternoon studying in preparation and praying for inspiration and guidance. Then I packed my suitcases for my early flight the next day. Maliheh prepared a very special Persian dinner which included chicken!

November 1: I was up by 5:30 AM, Breakfast (a glass of orange juice), was served and we were out the door for my 7 O'clock flight to Bangkok. What took 7 hours driving by car took 1 hour by air. Sunantha Smith met me at the airport and brought me to Nonthaburi Bahá'í Center. Both of us were exhausted so we went back to bed. She said she would call my room 1 hour before we were to leave at 12:30 PM for the Bangkok Bahá'í Center. My workshop was scheduled from 1:30 to 4:30 PM.

However, Sunantha over slept and arrived at my door minutes before our departure time... with no time for lunch. It couldn't be helped. By 3 PM my blood sugar was so low I feared that I would faint. I remembered my daughter's admonition to advocate for myself when necessary. So I stopped the workshop to ask if there were any crackers or cookies in the kitchen. A platter of juice and snacks soon arrived and I was refreshed enough to continue the workshop.

The day ended well with a good supper, a cool shower, a time to meditate and pray and sleeping in an air conditioned room.

November 2: This morning we visited Azar, a Persian woman, and her three children ages 5, 12, and 14. I remember that the 12 year old daughter asked interesting questions about wealth and poverty. She said that she thought God was unjust to create the world with poverty to begin with. This led into a very interesting discussion based on the Hidden Words of Bahá'u'lláh.

"O CHILDREN OF DUST! Tell the rich of the midnight sighing of the poor, lest heedlessness lead them into the path of destruction, and deprive them of the tree of wealth. To give and to be generous are attributes of mine; well is it which him that adorneth himself with My virtues."[2]

"O SON OF MY HANDMAID! Be not troubled in poverty nor confident in riches, for poverty is followed by riches, and riches are followed by poverty. Yet to be poor in all save God is a wondrous gift, belittle not the value thereof, for in the end it shall make thee rich in God, and thus thou shalt know the meaning of the utterance, "In truth ye are the poor," and the holy words, "God is the All-Possessing,"

---

[2] HWP #49

shall even as the true morn break forth gloriously resplendent upon the horizon of the lover's heart, and abide secure on the throne of wealth."[3]

We also consulted regarding 'Abdu'l-Bahá's quote in Paris Talks, p. 153, where He states, "Certainly, some being enormously rich and others lamentably poor, an organization is necessary to control and improve this state of affairs. It is important to limit riches, as it is also of importance to limit poverty. Either extreme is not good. To be seated in the mean is most desirable. If it be right for a capitalist to possess a large fortune, it is equally just that his workmen should have a sufficient means of existence."

"A financier with colossal wealth should not exist whilst near him is a poor man in dire necessity. When we see poverty allowed to reach a condition of starvation, it is a sure sign that somewhere we shall find tyranny. Men must bestir themselves in this matter, and no longer delay in altering conditions which bring the misery of grinding poverty to a very large number of the people. The rich must give of their abundance, they must soften their hearts and cultivate a compassionate intelligence, taking thought

---

[3] HWP #51

for those sad ones who are suffering from lack of the very necessities of life."

"There must be special laws made, dealing with these extremes of riches and want. The members of the government should consider the laws of God when they are framing plans for the ruling of the people. The general rights of mankind must be guarded and preserved."

"The government of the countries should conform to the Divine Law which gives equal justice to all. This is the only way in which the deplorable superfluity of great wealth and miserable, demoralizing, degrading poverty can be abolished. Not until this is done will the Law of God be obeyed."[4]

This was the meat of our discussion and while much of it was above the ability of the of the 12 year old daughter to understand, she seemed satisfied that the Baha'i Writings addressed the situation of poverty and wealth.

After this discussion Azar invited a woman named Ellie to have lunch with us. Ellie was involved in "energy work," a

---

[4] 'Abdu'l-Bahá, Paris Talks, p. 153

type of therapy that rebalances the energy system of the body to promote or facilitate healing. I was able to reassure Azar that this was a certified profession rather than an "occult" practice as she had been interpreting, and that I knew of several Bahá'ís who had been trained in this work, one of whom I had received treatment from. To clarify further, there are some certification programs in energy healing but state laws vary and that not all those who hold themselves out as practicing energy healing have a certification or legally need to. Ellie was also a great proponent of breastfeeding, had adopted two children as infants and had tried successfully to nurse them, which I learned was possible for some women.

I had to hurry back to the center for I was scheduled to teach two children's classes. I was always saying good-bye in Thailand, but this good-bye was reluctant as well as adventurous. Azar took me back to the center on the back of her motor bike. We crossed over small bridges and ditches where I had to dismount. We crossed busy roads, went up hill, downhill and I was in a dress hanging on for dear life.

The two children's classes were held at a private kindergarten at 2 PM. The first story I told was about the little bird that got stuck in my basement and how that relates to following the light of truth. The second story was about Truly the Elephant. It was a story of a family that starts their day with devotions and guidance about peace and love. The children then acted out what they learned during the class, followed by guidance in the evening devotions. The children then drew pictures about what they learned from the stories.

Soon I was back at the center, finishing up my packing, and Khun Jam Long, Naoko's chauffeur, arrived to pick me up for the two hour drive south to the Rayong area. But first we stopped at Mark and Neda's house where Naoko and her family were waiting. Then we were off to Naoko's favorite Japanese restaurant. Having come from a predominately fruitarian diet in Chiang Mai, I ate like a starving woman again, but the children's mischievous ways distracted me from my embarrassment. They crawled under the long, low table and tickled my feet while I pretended to protest. After 20 minutes of this I finally had to beg for mercy. Out from under the table three children popped. They came up behind me to massage my neck and shoulders. Then a fourth child trained a small hand-held, battery operated fan on my face. What a wonderful, special memory to carry home from Thailand. Children are truly the same all over the world.

November 3: Today is my husband, John's, birthday and I miss him greatly! I couldn't wait to present him with his opera glasses. By now I am counting the days and so is he. My energy is flagging today.

November 4: This had to be my most heart-breaking day. I taught "Protective Behaviors" to 19 children who were HIV positive. Across from the shelter where I taught is a 24 hour care facility for their mothers who have full blown AIDS, and next to that building is a hospice for those who are in the last stages of living/dying. There were gaunt children and rosy cheeked children, all of them on daily medication, all of them precious, all of their lives sacred.

The coloring sheets I handed out to them were a treasure to them. It helped me see very clearly the inordinate disparity between the rich and the poor and I felt shamed by my own materiality.

The Camilian Center is operated by a Catholic Social Service Agency. They are family oriented and strive to offer the children every opportunity to live life as fully as children who are not orphans. Since some of the children are quite weak, it is difficult for them to attend the local schools. The center provides literacy classes for everyone so they will be able to receive a formal education certificate. The children enjoy many outings that help them to develop a positive attitude, and improve their physical, psychological and intellectual well-being.

November 5: Today, too, was memorable. I taught at Huey Pong Institute, a government run orphanage with 150 children who have been abused, raped, abandoned, beaten and battered. I saw faces of children, purple and swollen, that made my heart cry out. I taught four classes of varying ages from 10 AM to 4 PM, without a bathroom break, with sweat pouring off of my back.

I was, however, afforded a brief respite at an outdoor restaurant, beneath towering pine trees on the beach a few miles from the orphanage. I was sure to load up on fluids, then forgot to use the ladies room before my afternoon classes. There was a cool breeze coming off of the sea and the temperature seemed at least 10 degrees cooler than just 5 miles inland. It showed me what a truly tropical paradise Thailand was.

A freeway divided the orphanage with males on one side and females on the other. I taught the young men in the afternoon and because the heat was extreme between 3 and 4 PM, even for the Thai people, and the staff departed during my class, the students misbehaved, went to sleep and were generally inattentive, the only experience like this that I had during my 35 days of teaching. Still I learned to plan ahead and state my needs for the next classes and require that staff and authority be present.

November 6: Naoko asked me if she could take the reins today. She wanted to try teaching "Protective Behaviors" to the second grade students at the Garden International School. She did an excellent job, so much so that she has plans to repeat this particular program to all the institutions at which I have taught 3 months from now as a refresher course. My energy has been flagging and now I am starting to feel sick.

November 7: I awoke at 3 AM with a very sore throat. I slept little that night. Naoko took over teaching the pre school children at the Garden International School. She easily adapted the program to the younger audience. I sneezed all day long. I have caught a cold from Jun, Naoko, Khun Ta (the maid), and Khun Jam Long, our driver. The children had a special celebration, with traditional Thai costume at school this evening, but because of my cold I decided to stay home and rest.

My cold was so bad I was worried about SARS. I e-mailed my husband and he said to just rest and not worry. He also said, "I want you to come home. Your mother wants you to come home. Sounds like you want to come home. Come Home!!" He always makes me laugh. I wrote back saying that I would be coming home soon.

November 8: Today is Saturday, a day off, and we went to the beach at 9:30 AM till 1 PM. I guarded the three older children in the shallow waters of the Gulf while Naoko shaded the baby from the fierce rays of the sun. The water was hot and the breeze was very cooling. We had rented lawn furniture and a table under the trees and at noon Naoko ordered a lunch consisting of tiny speckled hardboiled eggs, barbecued chicken, a spicy salad, and bright yellow watermelon.

I was warned that I should not use the public restrooms because they were so dirty. So I was happy that 1 O'clock was approaching because we were going to leave then. But as it happened we lingered till 2 PM and didn't get home until 3 PM, which meant that a restroom wasn't available for 6 hours. This happened frequently while I was in Thailand. Everyone was used to living like this, but I had never experienced it. I was thankful for two showers a day and sanitary napkins.

Before the children left school yesterday, they picked up boats 6 to 8 inches long that had been decorated with flowers for this evening's holiday celebration Each boat had a candle that would be lit before the children placed them on the shores of the Gulf of Bangkok, a body of water that reminds me of the vastness of Lake Michigan. It borders Cambodia.

It is said that the owner of the boat that floats the furthest out will receive good fortune throughout the year. This particular festival is in honor of the ancestors who have gone to the next world.

Jun's colleagues have prepared a beach party complete with roasted pig and giant, roasted in the shell fresh shrimp that are 10 inches or more long from antenna and head to tail. They were the best I've ever tasted in my life.

I gladly went to bed at 9 PM and slept 9 hours! A relief for my cold.

November 9: Today is Sunday. A day off. We did some shopping this afternoon and I will start filling up my extra box with gifts to take home with me. We went out for dinner this evening for fresh crab and fish that is exclusive to the Rayong area. I will truly miss the fresh seafood when I leave Thailand.

I have been nursing my sore throat since late last week trying to stay positive for I have 4 one hour programs to give at the Garden International School tomorrow. If I pace myself and don't force my voice, I should be able to make it.

November10: The Garden International School is British

owned and operated, teaching pre-school, plus K-12. Many countries are represented at the school because of the number of companies that bring in employees from all over the world. The fortunate thing for me is that they all spoke their native language plus English so I did not need a translator.

Today was a true joy because I could tell stories unencumbered and the subject was not as heavy as in the previous programs. The children were very responsive and laughed explosively in the appropriate places. In fact, they were so enchanted that 5 of the children came to Naoko's home that evening to beg me for more stories! Some of the older boys wanted a scary story, but as there were younger children present, I was hesitant to tell a story that would gross them out. So I pulled back some at the end so no one would have nightmares. The older boys were so unimpressed and disappointed. They went outside to play and I sat there trying to decide what if anything I could do. I decided to go out and ask the younger children to go inside for a little while. They really didn't want to but I was able to persuade them. Then I told the older boys an alternate ending to the scary story. Their eyes grew big and they were sufficiently grossed out and I kept my reputation as a good storyteller!   I still smile about it.

November 11: The Rayong Ladies Service Organization
met today for a coffee morning at which I gave a 30 minute
program on "Protective Behaviors for Children," including
statistics on child sexual abuse throughout the world. The
women from this group are deeply involved in the
development of the orphanage at which I taught on
November 5th. These movers and shakers of this small
community conduct many successful fundraisers; we're
talking hundreds of thousands of dollars, and have been
instrumental in actually upgrading dormitories that make
life more comfortable for the children.

They were highly interested in the information I gave them
and two of the ladies purchased my book, "Assisting the
Traumatized Soul: Healing the Wounded Talisman." One
of the ladies told me about Pattiya, a city with a population
of 100,000, 20,000 of which were in the sex trade industry.
She told me of a house party where young boys were
forced into a bathroom with older men. Confirmation of
the need for teaching Protective Behaviors and Boundaries
in Thailand.

November 12: Today we traveled to Sriraka where Mark
and Neda have organized my final presentation in Thailand
to the staff of a public elementary school. There are
perhaps 35 teachers present, plus the Principal of the
school. She graciously ushered us into her office where she
had some treats prepared in advance. My program had
come at an opportune time because they had just had to
remove a male teacher for sexually abusing a child.
Everyone was grateful to have the knowledge of prevention
and my handouts so they could present the program to the
children in my absence in the future. The Principal thanked
me for removing the veil from her eyes and from the eyes
of her staff. Two people in the group had flashbacks of
their former abuse and had to retire from the presentation to
the Principal's office to regain their composure. They
asked me for a private talk afterwards.

She then insisted on taking all six of us out for supper! The
restaurant was owned by one of her relatives and every dish
was superb. When I had taken what I thought was my last
bite, she insisted that I had to have dessert. I told her I just
couldn't eat anymore. She again insisted that I had to have
just one spoonful of a traditional Thai dessert. Oh, well,
just one spoonful! Little did I know that they would bring a

crushed ice that was covered with slightly sweetened coconut milk. It was so refreshing I quickly ate all of it! Of course, I didn't want to be rude. She was delighted.

November 13: Today was a day for organization. My box needed packing. Pictures needed to be picked up at the Kodak store. Suitcases needed reorganization. Things had to be discarded and left behind, and I needed some well earned rest. Naoko, Jun and Reiko and I stayed up till midnight talking and reliving the events of the last two weeks. Reiko is a wonderful friend of Naoko who came in from Japan for the last week of my visit. She also had arranged her return trip so that she would be on the same plane that I would be on.

November 14: I got to sleep in again today and this afternoon I had my last class at the Garden International School. Everything went well and one of the ladies of the Rayong Circle sat in because her daughter was in the class. It had to be moved to the library because the room Naoko usually reserved had to be used by others. Libraries are enchanting places and it was quite a distraction to some of the children, but we managed.

We were up late again tonight, talking, processing, and reviewing. All of us were anticipating the fact that we would soon be going our separate ways and that we would miss one another.

November 15: Not much to do today. I need to write a list of the things that are packed in my box for customs. Jun needs to seal it properly. I rested a lot today because I know how much of a strain tomorrow will be. I was actually able to sleep from 11 PM until 2 AM when Naoko awoke me. Khun Jam Long picked us up at 2:30 and we were on our way to the Bangkok International Airport.

November 16: We arrived at 5 AM and had to wait till 6:15 AM to get checked in. That left us 15 minutes to get to our gate. Boarding started at 6:30 AM and the flight left at 7:00. I slept all the way to Japan, made the plane change and slept a little more on the way to the U.S., arriving at Van Galder Bus Terminal in Rockford at 5 PM the same day. John arrived within 20 to 30 minutes and I was never so happy to see him. I was too tired to go out to eat so we just went home and I went to bed after making a few calls. It would take me five days to recover and weeks to process all of what I had experienced.

I could never have made this trip without the amazing ability of Naoko to coordinate my itinerary with the connections she had in the country of Thailand and I am so grateful to her.

I continued my correspondence with Marilyn Higgins. She informed me of a UNESCO Conference in China that was going to be held in the fall of 2005 and I applied to be a presenter. I asked John if he would like to accompany me and he said "Yes!" So we prepared for that.

PART TWO
Report on China and Japan
October 26 – November 16, 2005

October 26th: Departure from O'Hare on our way to the UNESCO 2005 International Forum on Education for Sustainable Development, where I was to offer a presentation on "Protective Behaviors for Children: Prevention of Exploitation." C.L. was my contact in Beijing, and also one of the coordinators of the conference. When I made my airline reservations in August, I planned to stay 5 extra days in China, then go on to Japan to give myself maximum amount of time to teach after the conference. Then 5 days before I left home I realized that I could contact C.L., which I did, to see if she knew of other venues, schools, organizations, where I could teach my program. She e-mailed me the name and e-mail address of S.Y. in North Eastern Beijing, who asked for a short bio to pass along to her contacts. Thus my reach was extended.

Thursday, October 27th: Arrival at Beijing International Airport at 2:30 PM. The Hotel had a van ready to pick us up so that transition went smoothly. However, we did not understand the Hotel's method of charging us ahead of time an exorbitant fee for services not rendered yet, so there was some difficulty in communication when we registered. We went to bed early (7:30-8:00 PM) so that we could become acclimated as quickly as possible.

Friday, October 28th: Today was essentially a free day as the registration for the conference did not start until 4 or 5 PM. My husband, John, and friend from Yamaguchi, Japan, Marilyn Higgins, did some sightseeing to the Forbidden City and to Silk Street. The Forbidden City was our first introduction to the history of China and there were a lot of people there. We had an opportunity to chat with a couple, one Chinese, the other American. We ate lunch from a vendor at the Forbidden City, who sold boiled noodles with beef.

We used an audio guide system for much of the tour and things were also labeled in English and Chinese.

We got back in time for registration and tried to work out, with the conference coordinator, our unhappiness about the overcharging of our room, to no avail.

Dinner was at 6:00 PM during which time the foreign guests/presenters were introduced to one another.

Saturday, October 29th: The Conference opened at the Conference Center for the National School of Administration in the Hai Dian District of Beijing, with children singing. There were welcome speeches, plus 16 Keynote speeches, one of which was given by our friend, Dr. D.A., who spoke on Sustainable Teacher Improvement.

A banquet was prepared for the evening where all of the Chinese guests/participants as well as the foreign presenters were included. This was a lavish event with a dozen or more courses plus wine and many toasts (of which we did not partake).

Sunday, October 30th: Today six different sessions ran concurrently all day long and I was able to both present my program and sit in on several others. In the last two days, I was able to perceive that this Conference was very heavy on "Environmental Development" rather than presenting a balanced view of what is needed worldwide for sustainable development with a multi-faceted view.

I was asked to sit in on the youth session by one of the conference coordinators, because the youth wanted the view points of foreigners in attendance. I was thrilled to hear about the research these youth had done regarding how to save the environment. They presented their power point in Chinese and then explained in English the same presentation. I found the energy completely different in the youth sessions and thought them quite brilliant in their consultation.

My own program was well received. I handed out copies of my workshop to the approximately 40 people in attendance. I had 30 minutes to give a presentation which had to be translated so that left me 15 minutes to get my points across. The translator appeared to be uncomfortable and embarrassed because my topic was about sexuality, but he bravely overcame that, followed me out of the room when I finished and asked me for my business card because he was highly interested in the subject of Protective Behaviors for Children.

Monday, October 31st: Today the group went to visit different schools studying about the environment, but my husband and I went to the Temple of Heaven[5] and back to Silk Street.

Tuesday, November 1st: This was the closing day of the Conference with presentations of awards to schools and individuals and experimental schools that had made great achievements in Education for Sustainable Development. All of the foreign presenters and the plenary speaker were given 5 minutes to present closing thoughts about the conference.

Afternoon: Great Wall and the Jade carving establishment. John and I enjoyed climbing the Great Wall and took pictures of that event.

Wednesday, November 2nd: Today my husband left to return to the U.S. It is our good fortune that he was accompanied to Chicago by M.G. They were able to sit next to one another on the flight. M. has a hip disability and my husband was able to assist him at both airports.

---

[5] The **Temple of Heaven** (Chinese: 天坛; pinyin: Tiāntán; Manchu: Abkai mukdehun) is an imperial complex of religious buildings situated in the southeastern part of central **Beijing**. The complex was visited by the Emperors of the Ming and Qing dynasties for annual ceremonies of prayer to **Heaven** for good harvest

My husband left at noon and by 12:15 I was picked up by
Ms. H.S., the owner and director of New Century
Kindergarten Group, which oversees the development of
over 2000 pre-school students.

She, and the interpreter she provided, drove me to her site
where I presented "Protective Behaviors for Children:
Prevention of Exploitation" (Training the Trainers) to 40
teachers and principals. Each of them received a copy of
the handouts for the program so that they could duplicate it
in their classroom. They have plans to translate my
program into Chinese.

Protective Behaviors for Children

Training the Trainers

I.   Introduction:

My name is Phyllis Peterson and I am a survivor
of incest from the ages of 2 through 8 years old.
The effects of this abuse have lasted for a life
time because these were my developmental
years in which sexuality and immorality was
approved by a perpetrator that was the most
important authority figure in my life. I was a
sexualized child which, I believe, led to my

becoming bi-polar and acting out sexually as a teenager and adult.

This excerpt from my book "Assisting the Traumatized Soul: Healing the Wounded Talisman," shows you where I was 20 years ago: Please don't look too closely at me. You might see my secret. Please don't talk to me. I might accidentally tell you my secret. No, I don't want to be friends. Friends tell secrets. No, I don't want that promotion. I'm too occupied with my secret. And I can't express an opinion either. You might guess my secret. No, I'm not going to invite you to my home. We have a houseful of secrets! What's the sense of sharing feelings? People with secrets avoid them. And no, I can't tell you what my secret is. It's so secret, I may not be fully conscious of it.[6]

Being able to tell my secret hundreds of times within the safety of a support group helped to validate my experience and helped me to recognize that it was not my fault. Most survivors of incest believe, incorrectly that they were responsible for the abuse. Nothing could be farther from the truth.

My journey has led through a series of miss-diagnoses, wrong medication and a skewed perception of what life is truly meant to be....to a life that is fulfilling and creative, with relationships that are loving and trusting. In order for this to happen, I had to define and

---

[6] Phyllis K. Peterson, "Assisting the Traumatized Soul: Healing the Wounded Talisman", Baha'i Publishing Trust, © 1999, page 5.

discover a just, nurturing authority and the importance of obedience to authority. I had to lead that sexualized child to grow and develop morally through a process of education. I wish that my education on sexual boundaries had begun when I was at least 3 years old. I am one of the fortunate ones. I did receive an education and I attribute that education...and my growing faith and ever developing morality to the teachings of a great philosopher who taught me to follow higher principles.

Throughout my journey of healing I have attended many conferences on Child Abuse. I am here today to teach you what I have learned about how to protect children by making them aware of sexual boundaries. I am not a therapist but I can teach prevention. I can teach parents and children how to be aware of sexual boundaries. And I can train you in how to teach awareness of physical boundaries to children as young as 3 years old, children who are old enough to sit still and listen to a story and enjoy arts and crafts. There are simple techniques that can equip a child with acute awareness. And just as we repeat to children the need for manners on a regular basis, so too, we need to follow up and reinforce the teachings of physical boundaries on a regular basis. So I encourage you to take notes so that you can repeat these techniques as you see a need for them.

II.   Why is prevention important?

We know the horrific statistics on sexual abuse of children. Here are some facts and figures from the United States. One in four females is molested in childhood. One in seven boys is molested before the age of 18. 150,000 to 200,000 new cases of sexual abuse are being reported each year. In England a quarter of all rape victims are children.

In South Africa the largest group of perpetrators (33%) was school teachers. The findings suggest that child rape is becoming more common, and lend support to qualitative research of sexual harassment of female students in schools in Africa. South Africa has one of the highest rates of rape in the world, mostly against children. Every half an hour, a child is sexually abused in Brazil. Sometimes by Brazilians, sometimes by foreigners, who are presented the children by an intermediary who has rented them by the day from their families.

Regarding sexual violence against children in Eastern Europe, Sexual violence against young boys and girls up to 15 years old accounts for 30 per cent of all crimes in this category, and it is most often children between 8 and 12 years old who are attacked. The perpetrators are known to their victims in 50 per cent of cases, and roughly 40 per cent of crimes of this kind are committed by relatives. The enormity of the problem can be realized by the fact that in India alone, at least 25 percent of the adult population has been molested before the age of 16. At least 27 million females are adult survivors of child sexual abuse. In Thailand it is estimated that up to 200,000 children have been sold into sexual slavery. It is a multi-national, multi-billion dollar industry in cities like Pattaya. These are but samples of a world wide problem that should have all of us working on it. The sexual abuse of children is everyone's business and we must be about how to remedy it.[7]

We also know that immoral, degenerate or ignorant people prey upon the fact that children and their caregivers are not aware. Perpetrators seek out the compliant child. Sadly, some of our youth are acting out the immorality that they have been taught. Power over one's body and path in life starts with knowledge. Remarkably, the moral education of children can start very young. Not only does it include teaching children virtues such as kindness, compassion, love, understanding and friendship, but it includes knowledge of personal boundaries.

The workshop entitled "Protective Behaviors for Children" is a one hour *preventive* workshop that teaches children how to be aware of boundaries for the private areas of their bodies *before* someone does something that is inappropriate or harmful. The program incorporates all of the senses, the different ways of knowing, plus the power of speech to help children fully retain what is learned.

Participants in this workshop will learn how to teach children to ask for help, who to ask, how to conquer their fears and how to say NO, STOP, and HELP! They will learn to be aware of three different types of touch: Gentle touch, hurting touch and secret touch. Moreover,

---

[7] These statistics were taken from the Internet. Simply go to Google and explore by putting in (Country) and the words "child sexual abuse."

this is a vital language skill for the morally educated child. For how else would they be able to define or describe what has happened?

One of the most instinctive virtues a child, even a baby, has is empathy. Perpetrators prey upon this and prey upon the unaware, compliant child. What you can do is teach children to not be compliant in specific situations.

There is a simple song everyone will learn, plus arts and crafts such as the "Fear-A-Lizer" with which they learn to pulverize their fears. They can make a Magic Warrior Shield (made from a simple paper plate or the handout pattern at the back of this paper) that reinforces where internal and external confidence comes from. (*Internal* being the special strengths each individual child has and *external* referring to the system of support that surrounds the child – parents, village mentors, counselors, professionals, etc.) There are two coloring sheets and an outline that will be provided for each participant in this workshop so that attendees such as children, parents, grandparents, babysitters, teachers, therapists, counselors and trainers can have tools to take home with them enabling them to demonstrate the program in their own locality. There is no cost for these tools.

The Protective Behaviors for Children workshop has been presented to schools, orphanages, and Catholic Social Service Agencies in Thailand as well as in Japan, China and the United States. Staff training has also been conducted so that teachers can follow up 3 months or so later.

III. When my grandson, Tanner, was 3 years old, he asked my daughter-in-law, "Who made all the people in the world?" She answered, "God (or a Supreme Being)." Then he asked, "But who made all the bad people?" She answered, "God made all the people and allowed them to make choices, but some people chose to do bad things." A Great Educator that has taught me said that "The root cause of wrong doing is ignorance." So we have a need to educate both the wrong doer for the protection of society and to educate those who are innocent. The following is one method of teaching children to be aware of boundaries.

1. Opening: What children will learn:
   a. How to ask for help
   b. Who to ask for help
   c. How to conquer their fears
   d. That they have permission to say NO! STOP! And HELP!
2. There are three kinds of touch: Gentle touch, hurting touch and secret touch. Describe them. Pat yourself on the arm or cheek very gently to demonstrate gentle touch; pinch yourself and say "OUCH!"to illustrate hurting touch. You can also use a doll or a stuffed animal to give the children a visual image of gentle touch, rocking the doll or stuffed animal. You can also speak of bullies at school or in the neighborhood and the types of behaviors that they exhibit, such as hitting, kicking, punching, twisting arms, and other types of fighting
3. Ask them: "Where are your private places?" And then tell them, "Anywhere you can cross your arms on your body. No one is allowed to do hurting touch or secret touch there. Secret touch

is when someone tries to put their hands under your clothing or inside your panties and tells you not to tell Mommy or Daddy (or the authorities)". Talk about people who are trying to do good for them such as a Doctor or a Nurse and differentiate when it is appropriate. Babies and small children, for example, need help with cleaning their private areas and the changing of their diapers. Remember that 80% of cases of sexual abuse are done by family members and therefore the child has to be told that Mommy and Daddy cannot do secret touch, too. Hand out pictures #1 through #4 to demonstrate the following.

    a. Face: Have the children (or workshop participant) cross their arms over their face as the boy is doing in picture #1. Talk about the feelings they would have if someone did hurting touch there. Tell them. "No one can touch your face without your permission. Unless they have a good reason to help you." (Don't have them start coloring here yet. Just talk about the pictures and ask them questions about the picture. Ask them what they think the boy is feeling.)

    b. Chest: Cross arms over the chest as the girl is doing in picture #2. Talk about the feelings they might have if someone touched them there. Tell them, "No one can touch your chest without your permission." Ask them what they think the girl is feeling.

    c. Pelvic area or genitals: Cross arms over their pelvis. Talk about the feelings they perceive on the boy's face in the picture. Tell them, "No one has the right to touch your genitals without your permission." (We will discuss later on what they can say verbally. Because we are an international group and because the children you will teach are at different developmental stages, know that you must choose wording that is familiar to their experience and your locality. You don't have to be limited to this language. You can be creative.)

d. Buttocks: Have them cross their arms over their buttocks. Again, talk about the feelings the little girl in the picture might have or they might have. If you have a mixed group of boys and girls, don't forget to address this issue with the boys, even though there is a girl in picture #4. So it is with all of the pictures.

A word on "Feelings"...children can be taught at a very young age to express their feelings. Feeling language can be very difficult even for adults. To give you an example, I was present when my niece came screaming into a room where all the family was gathered for a holiday. We did not know what was wrong, but my sister held her and said, "Tell Momma, I'm frightened of the helicopter! Tell Momma, I'm frightened." She was teaching her feeling language at 2 and ½ years old. It's as necessary as teaching a child manners and boundaries. The words for feelings in English are on the coloring sheet and there are lines for which the children can write out their own feelings in their own language.

4. Song: This is My Private Place. If you are a musical person and like to sing, make up your own tune to the following words. And if you are not a musical person, just teach them to recite the words like a chant, a nursery rhyme or a poem. I will sing it for you:

> This is my private place. (Cross arms over the face.)
>
> This is my private place. (Cross arms over the chest.)
>
> This is my private place. (Cross arms over the pelvis.)
>
> One, Two, Three, and Four!
>
> When you say "one", demonstrate by crossing arms over the face.
>
> When you say "two", demonstrate by crossing arms over the chest.
>
> When you say "three", demonstrate by crossing arms over the pelvis.
>
> Then quickly turn around and slap both hands on your buttocks saying,
>
> "And four!"

After you have demonstrated it for them two or three times, have them stand up and sing it, going through the motions. You are, in fact, teaching them through movement, motion, music, speech and visualization.

5. Now, hand out the coloring crayons or markers and have them color the pictures. This will be the third or fourth time you have gone through these concepts with them which will help fix it in their memories. Walk around the room from table to table or desk to desk and encourage them and review the information as you acknowledge each one of them individually. Say things like:

What a good job you are doing.

I like the way you color.

Can you tell what feelings are in his or her heart by the expression on the face?

You have a special way of coloring.

What's your favorite color?

Do you like to color at home and at school?

(Translate what feeling words are written in English for each picture. If they can write, have them write the feeling words in Chinese, Thai, Japanese, German, Indian, the African languages, etc.)

6. Ask the children "Have you ever felt embarrassed, afraid or ashamed? Did your stomach hurt?" "What are your favorite foods?" "What foods make you feel sick in your stomach?" "That sick feeling can be called a yuckie feeling. Secret touch can make you feel many different types of feelings which are like warning signs." "If you feel yuckie, uncomfortable or ashamed when someone does secret touch, it's not because of something you did, but because of what THEY did. What I want you to do is run away as fast as you can. That yuckie feeling is a RED FLAG that tells you something is not right and you need to run to someone who is safe and tell them what happened. You can also tell the person who is making you feel uncomfortable 'NO! Stop that! I don't like it when you do that!'"[8] Next we will learn how to teach them to ask for help and who to ask for help if they couldn't run away.

7. Hand out the picture of the hand and the pencils. If you do not have the picture of the hand, you can make one by simply placing your hand on a blank sheet of paper and tracing around your fingers and your thumb and making copies. Or have the children trace around their own hands on a blank piece of paper. There is a sample provided with this paper.

   Have them write NO! STOP! And HELP in large letters or characters in the palm of the hand or

---

[8] This phrase was adapted from Sandy Kleven, LCSW, The Right Touch, Illumination Arts Publishing Company, Inc. Bellevue, Washington. This is a read-aloud story to help prevent child sexual abuse.

write it for them if they are too young, teaching them what the words mean. Have safe scissors ready. Tell the children "To stop hurting touch and secret touch you have to be able to tell someone who is safe, someone you can trust, someone who would only do something good for you and to you." Then ask them "Who is a safe person? Who would you ask to help you? Who would listen to you and believe you?"

Start with the thumb and have them write in a name of someone who is safe...Mom or Dad, for instance. If it is Mom or Dad who is perpetrating the abuse, ask for another name. Go on to the pointer finger (the first finger) and ask them who else can they think of that is safe who would never do secret touch or hurting touch. Have them write in the name of whoever they can think of. They may say Auntie, Grandmother. Move on to the second finger and ask again. If they are having difficulty thinking up people, make suggestions such as brother, cousin, friend. Do the same with the third and fourth fingers, suggesting Doctor, policeman, nurse, or teacher. One boy in an orphanage in Thailand said he would call in the army!

Have them color the hand red and cut it out with safe scissors. Red is a universal color for STOP! Have them raise their paper hands together and shout out as a group "NO! STOP! HELP!" Raising the hand is also a universal sign for HELP!

If you are in a class room situation, all the hands of the children can be placed on a bulletin board to remind them of this exercise. Attention can be drawn to the bulletin board after a two week period has passed and the techniques can be reviewed.

Then tell them, "If the person on the thumb doesn't listen, tell the person on the pointer finger. If that person doesn't listen, tell the person on the next finger, and the next, and keep telling until someone listens. Don't stop! Be brave! Keep telling and telling and telling and don't stop!"

8. Skills and Tools:

Bravery and courage come from having skills and tools. Children become fearful and compliant because they are either unaware of what is happening or they don't know what to do. The equipment you will need for this part of the workshop are crackers, plastic bags, scotch tape, markers and a rolling pin or other long round object (like a tall glass or a long 1 inch wooden dowel) that can crush the cracker that is in the plastic bag. The following list of skills should be written on slips of paper. Each child will tape the skills to the rolling pin or tall glass or even a piece of wood. Be creative. Have at least three or four different slips of paper for each child.

    a. I know what hurting touch and secret touch are.
    b. I can run away as fast as I can

c. I can yell for help and say NO! STOP! And Help!

d. I'm a quick thinker!

e. I'm a smart and brave kid.

f. I know ahead of time who to ask for help!

g. I can tell 5 people and keep telling until someone listens.

h. I can say "Stop that! I don't like it when you do that!"

i. I know my body belongs to me and nobody can touch it.

After all of the children have read their skills aloud, tape them with the scotch tape to the rolling pin or cylindrical object. Then hand out the crackers, plastic bags and wide-tip Sanford Markers. Have them write FEAR on the cracker and put the cracker in the plastic bag, sealing it shut. Now one at a time, have them crush their fear with their powerful skills that are taped to the rolling pin, telling them "Look how strong you are! You know what to say and do! Good for you! You can conquer your fears because you have special powers." Say the verbal skills out loud again to all of them. These skills give them powers. Tell them that they can take their plastic bags home with them, open them when they are outside and let the wind blow all the cracker crumbs away, releasing their fears. Be sure to have extra crackers so that the children can have a treat to celebrate this moment. Do warn them not to eat the cracker that they have written on with the marker because it has chemicals on it.

9. Every country has its Warriors! The next craft project you will teach the children to make is a Magic Warrior Shield. The pattern for it is attached to the back of this paper. You should copy it onto card stock or card board that is thin enough to cut out. The strip on the bottom is to be stapled to the back so they can slip their hand into it and hold it in front of themselves as a Magic Warrior Shield. (You could also use paper plates if they are available in your country.) Hand out pencils, markers and a stapler or two.

   a. Have them draw a picture on the Shield of someone who would protect them, such as parents, the family dog, a policewoman or a doctor. One child asked me to draw an attack cat on hers! This is their outside help (external guidance).
   b. Tell them to write NO! STOP! HELP! On the inside of the Shield. This is their personal, inside strength.
   c. If there are any of the SKILLS left over from the previous project, have them tape some to the inside. Discuss these skills out loud as they work, telling them that they have the personal power of a Warrior.

10. There are three more important points to teach the children.

a. They have to tell one of the five people on their hand even if the person doing the secret touch says they will harm someone the child loves. Sex offenders count on the fear of the child as their ally. They count on the child being unaware and powerless. This workshop teaches children what to do ahead of time. This is prevention before it happens, before the abuse is buried, so that the child will have the opportunity to talk things out.

b. The children must be taught that if someone does secret touch, it is not the fault of the child. Some children think that it is their fault and that may keep them from saying something out loud. So tell them over and over throughout the work shop, "It would not be your fault."

c. The final concept to bring before them is this: "Nothing that can happen to you is so terrible that you can't say it out loud to someone you trust." Have them say it out loud to you, too. "Nothing that can happen to me is so terrible that I can't say it out loud to someone I trust."

11. Now, have them stand up and repeat the song: "This is my Private Place!

This is my private place! (Cross arms over face.)

This is my private place! (Cross arms over chest.)

This is my private place! (Cross arms over pelvis.)

One, two, three, and four!

(On one cross arms over face, on two cross arms over chest, on three cross arms over pelvis, and on four turn your back to them and slap your hands on your buttocks.)

IV. Closing

In the book, "The Right Touch", author Sandy Kleven makes several very good suggestions on how to get help for the child and how to rectify the situation. If a child comes to you and tells you that someone has touched them inappropriately, BELIEVE THE CHILD! Give the child plenty of reassurance that it was right to tell and that it was not his or her fault. Remember that you are not qualified to confront the accused offender, so you must turn it over to the authorities. You can request assistance from the police, sheriff, or a child protection agency.

I know that we have many countries represented here today, so I couldn't begin to know the many agencies that are and are not available to you. I can give you an example from the United States. There is a Childhelp USA Hotline at 1-800-4-A-Child that has trained counselors available 24 hours a day for crisis intervention. They can also offer referrals to counseling agencies and support groups. They offer literature upon request. Children and adults may be connected to counselors in 144 languages as needed.

Ms. Kleven says you can also use the Internet to find a vast network of resources to help deal with this unfortunate but all-too-common problem that is an epidemic world wide. The Childhelp USA site is a good place to start: www.childhelpusa.org or you can e-mail them at help@childhelpusa.org.[9]

What else can you do? You can recognize that this is a community problem as well as a world wide problem, not an individual problem. You can start a support group with the women and men in your community, teaching this work shop on a regular basis in order to empower both the children and the adults. Adult mothers who have not received counseling for their own abuse are known to not have good boundaries and skills and awareness to prevent this injustice happening to their own children.

If we go back to the statistics, say in India alone where at least 27 million adult females have experienced child sexual abuse, imagine the percentage that don't have good boundaries or awareness to protect their own children so it becomes a generational problem that could have been prevented with education for sustainable development.

When I was teaching protective behaviors in Thailand to a group of teachers, a woman approached

[9] Sandy Kleven, "The Right Touch", © 1997, Illumination Arts Publishing Company, Inc., Bellevue, Washington.

me after my talk. She said that a four year neighbor boy had forced her 2 year old grand daughter into the oral sex position on his body. She didn't know what to do. She was afraid of offending his father who was a well respected man in town. Yet she did not know how to interpret the boy's behavior...if it was something he had seen in the home or on TV, she couldn't be sure...but she felt a great need to protect her grand daughter.

I told her it was time for her to rise up to leadership in her community and act as though this was a community problem not an individual problem. She could gather the adults and children in her community to teach them the concepts in this workshop to create awareness as a preventive measure and continue to teach her grand child through the years to protect her. That way she would not have to point a finger at any individual, but enlighten the entire community.

At one time I was at a conference in New York City when a woman revealed to me that she allowed a trusted male friend to baby-sit her 6 year old daughter while she attended a meeting. Her husband was out of town. When she returned home and her friend, a member of her church, had left, she started putting her daughter to bed. It was then that her daughter said, "I hope Mr. Smith never touches me again like he did tonight."

Her mother's heart was in her throat! But she remained calm. "Where did Mr. Smith touch you?" The little girl said, "Right here," pointing to her pubic area. The first thing her mother did was believe her child. Then she said, "How did it make you feel?" The little girl said, "Yuckie!" Her mother asked her, "Do you want to talk about it?" The little girl said, "No, not right now, I just want to go to bed." "Well," said her mother, "If you want to talk about it later, I have a special friend who is really good about talking about such things and we'll go and see her. But I want you to know that it wasn't your fault that Mr. Smith did that and you will never have to be alone with him again."

Then she tucked her daughter in bed and went to her room and screamed into her pillow. The next morning she called Mr. Smith. Fortunately she had recently learned how to create an I-Statement, so she formed her words very carefully to that format.

And she said, "Mr. Smith, I want you to know that I feel very angry that you touched my daughter in an inappropriate way and I want to know what you plan to do so that you will never touch another child in this way and so that you will stop losing friends and to correct your behavior in the future? I know that you were to come to my house for a meeting this weekend, but you are no longer welcome in my home. You are never to see my daughter again because I think that would be detrimental to her healing." Mr. Smith stumbled over his words, said as he wept that he was sorry and that he would get some help.[10]

Today that little girl is about 16 to 18 years old and is whole and healthy because she felt safe enough to communicate this out loud to her mother and the incident wasn't buried without discussion and support. She was told that it was not her fault and she was protected from ever being alone with this man again.

---

[10] Phyllis Peterson, Assisting the Traumatized Soul, © 1999, Baha'i Publishing Trust, Wilmette, IL, p. 133

Imagine though, if her mother had been able to follow up and teach her the skills in this workshop, to reinforce these concepts.

Here is one last story and then I will open the program up to questions and discussion. I may not be able to answer all the questions, but together as a group I am sure we will find suggestions and solutions that will expand our knowledge on this very important subject.

A more subtle but dangerous form of abuse:

One year when I was traveling from city to city in Wisconsin, my hostess in one home greeted me at the door. Her three year old daughter was at her side. Susan, a former social worker, explained to me that Frances did not like to be hugged or touched. I was very impressed with the fact that this mother was immediately setting boundaries for me in order to support her daughter's feelings and preferences. I always make a point of allowing a child to come to me rather than me forcing myself onto a child. Children sense who is to be trusted and if left to themselves will test the water so to speak.

I was there to demonstrate my "Boundary Sculpting Game" which creates consciousness of what we do unconsciously instead of setting clear boundaries with others. Susan invited many of her neighbors and there were plenty of people participating in the game. After the game I provided time for discussion and memories of times we had either crossed the boundaries of others or they had crossed our boundaries.

Susan revealed an interesting problem that was confronting her at family holiday gatherings. Her family knew was Frances' preferences were, yet Susan's brother would tease and cajole Frances to hug him even though she consistently told him "No!" Then he would make a game out of it, trying to turn her NO into a YES! He would work away at her until finally she acquiesced. Then the entire family would laugh.

Susan would be very disturbed but did not have support in putting her brother in his place, at a safe distance from Frances. She was also afraid of rocking the boat and ruining family gatherings by setting rigid boundaries, or being thought of as rigid. What was really happening was this: In Susan's brother's eyes, Frances' no did not mean NO!

Now, many of us who work with youth, teenagers and women who have been raped on dates, know that their NO did not mean NO to the rapist. Susan's daughter was in a precarious situation in the developmental years of her life. And after playing "The Boundary Sculpting Game", Susan had finally found the key, the language, and the concepts to verbalize what was actually going on within this situation.

Through the group discussion that we had, Susan decided that she had to firmly tell her brother "No!" and that if he did not respond appropriately to her authority as Frances' mother, then she would not attend family gatherings until he did.

Remember, the greatest need with Protective Behaviors for Children is to empower them with knowledge of how to say NO and to support them with awareness of boundaries for the private areas of their bodies. Next they need the skills for asking for help. They need to be told that it was not their fault. And if upon hearing that the child has been abused, the child must be assured that they are believed. Ask questions about their feelings, teach them the feeling language. There are over 250 feeling words in the English language. Use every opportunity to help children to express their feelings from the youngest age possible. And please also remember that you must turn it over to qualified authorities when someone has done something to break the law. There are laws against child sexual abuse and you may not have the authority to confront the individual or enforce the law.

And so I finish the program with these final words that can be said to the child, which you will have them repeat back to you three times:

There is nothing that can happen to you that is so terrible that you can't say it out loud to someone you trust.

Thank you for coming today and thank you so much for caring.   Questions and discussion. Handouts attached.

** Excerpts from "Assisting the Traumatized Soul" used by Permission of the National Spiritual Assembly of the Baha'is of the United States.

Thursday, November 3rd: At 12:00 Noon I was picked up by S.Y., Director of Character Education Program for the

Family Learning House. I taught the Protective Behaviors Workshop for a group of 25 teachers, parents and principals, leaving them with the entire program and copies of the handouts. Shiva was present when I gave my program at the UNESCO conference and was also my contact for all of these daycare/preschool owners and directors, setting things up for me when I was in the U.S. as well as in China.

At 3:00 PM I was picked up for a program to be presented for D. V. at Daystar Academy. She is directing a wonderful program for children. There were 30 teachers, parents and principals present and I, again, presented my program. Everywhere I went the teachers were eager to learn and asked many questions through the interpreter. Two months before my arrival a parent went to D., the Director, telling her that she was concerned about "abuse" issues, pointing to D. and saying "What are YOU going to do about it?" Dawn told me later that my coming was an answer to prayer because she had been saying, "All I need is a program. All I need is a program. I can do it if I only had a program!" Two weeks later I walk in with a program! God is good!!

At the close of this presentation I began talking about the program I was going to give in Japan titled, "The Importance of the Development of Feelings in the Child and the Adult" and that I had a list of "feeling" words to teach verbal skills and vocabulary to young children. They were so disappointed that they were going to miss out on this workshop and its handouts that I told them I would e-mail all of it to them as soon as I returned to the states. Indeed, I sent the complete program to all of my contacts in China when I came home.

S.Y. lived in the neighborhood of this school and invited me to her home for dinner, where we had an informal talk. It was a lovely Persian meal and I was very grateful for it. Two important people were there. Ms. M. C., an English woman who is an AMI Montessori Directress for the Family Learning House. Also, B.J., who is a Chinese Teacher, ESL Teacher, an Interpreter and Translator. B.J. is very troubled. She was raped twice when she was 15 years old and her daughter, at 4 years old was groomed by an older man for abuse purposes. B.J. is troubled because she has been diagnosed as being bi-polar and she is delaying getting the help she needs for one reason after another. I am hoping that the time I spent with her will be helpful to her in making a decision to reach out for help. I didn't have an extra book with me (My new one "Healing the Wounded Soul") at the dinner, but had one at my hotel that I was planning to take to Japan. Upon my return to my hotel I decided it was right to give it to B.J. and then send another book by mail to Japan when I returned home.

I went home to my hotel and said the long healing prayer for B.J. and made arrangements with her to meet me Friday afternoon. When I returned to the Hotel, I saw C.L. who informed me that I barely got into the country, because the vice-president of the Beijing Academy of Educational Sciences was afraid of my topic and did not want to allow me in the Conference!

Friday, November 4th: I went to see the great Bell Temple[11] Northwest of the Huang Yuan Hotel on my own in a taxi and felt such freedom to know that I could negotiate my way in China on a limited basis, it was under construction and it was expected that I would pay to take

---

[11] Newly refurbished, this famous shrine (originally called Juéshēng Temple) was once a pit stop for Qing emperors who came here to pray for rain.

pictures of the Great Bell that weighed 40 tons. It would cost more to hit it with a mallet.

I declined and decided to sit in the courtyard with my journal in the sunshine, going into a meditative mood, However, the caretaker decided to put on a show for me. She hit the mallet slowly up to 15 times which resonated like a deep Ohmmm that could be heard for 25 miles. Then she turned on an audio tape that played flute and bell music that was just enchanting. There I was basking in the sunlight in a prayerful, meditative state with all my cares floating away. I was extremely grateful. The bell cast in bronze had a raised surface, it was covered with 22 thousand sutras which show what a work of art and spirituality it was. When it was first cast, they were unable to move it, until a couple of hundred years passed and another emperor took the throne. He thought of the idea of digging a giant ditch or canal in the winter time, then having his men filling it with water until it froze and then sliding the bell down the ditch to its final resting place.

B.J. came this afternoon and we talked and had tea in my room. We talked about bi-polar illness, how hard it is to sit and wait all day long to be seen to get medication in the first place, how she loses a day of work when she goes to the hospital, how she cannot sustain a job, yet she doesn't believe China can sustain her needs. Her method is to run from place to place when things go wrong. She has some advocates and I implored her to trust in and turn to them. I gave her my book under great protest for she knew it was promised to someone in Japan. I reassured her that I felt right in giving it to her. She left my presence in an uplifted state.

Saturday, November 5th: At 3:00 PM Mr. L., a Principal at "The Little Adults" School, who has a Master's Degree in Psychology, picked me up for a 4 O'clock program. He brought an interpreter along to translate.

B.J. called me and wanted to have one more evening with me, so we went out to eat at a lovely Chinese restaurant and I had the best Chinese food I had had since I had been there. It was dim sum with pork and leek. This outing gave me a third strong opportunity to urge her to hang in there and keep trying to get some help. She reads English well so my book should be of great benefit to her.

Sunday, November 6th: Today is packing day. I leave the Huang Yuan Hotel tomorrow at 11:00 AM for the Beijing International Airport. I had no appointments so I spent most of the day in the coffee shop in the lobby of the hotel in case I might meet someone to talk to. What was left of the conference presenters had departed yesterday.

After dinner I spent the rest of the evening organizing my luggage, preparing for tomorrow's trip and praying for protection.

JAPAN

Monday, November 7th: I started checking out of the hotel around 10 AM and that went smoothly. My flight left at 2:50 PM and I arrived at 7:15 PM at Narita Airport in Japan.

This was the part that I felt unsure of. Somehow I had to get through Customs, quarantine, immigration, money exchange, baggage, and find the Japan Rail to Yokohama with my luggage and by the grace of God before 9 PM! Divine Assistance comes through every time!

Making it to the correct platform, I met a Japanese family that was going to Yokohama, and who guided me through the maze of the Tokyo station, when we had to change trains for Yokohama. Once there I waited for 30 minutes for Naoko Kagami, who would be my hostess for three days. It was now 12:40 AM and we had yet to board another train to Fujisawa. Naoko tucked me into my hotel next door to her home at 1:30 AM.

Tuesday, November 8th: I slept in then went next door to Naoko's home for breakfast and at 4 PM Naoko started her neighborhood Virtues class in the basement of her apartment building. There were 15 children and four parents present while we played games, I told stories, and Naoko taught them English language skills and virtues.

Wednesday, November 9th: A Baha'i woman, Mitsuko Yamamoto, arrived from south of Yamaguchi and at 10 AM we had a women's meeting where I gave a talk on Unity in the Community. Five women were present. One or two were not Bahá'í but were very interested in the Faith. They were especially interested in the topic of "anger" and how to express it in an appropriate way, yet still maintain unity.

Thursday, November 10th: We left Naoko's home at 2 PM for my presentation at her children's elementary school, where there were 75 parents, teachers, principals and representatives from 3 more elementary schools. My topic was "The Importance of the Development of Feelings in Young Children through Adulthood." I taught them that we have two natures…a spiritual nature and a material, physical nature. And that love and virtues are like an umbrella that governs all of our feelings so that they can be directed and regulated by our higher, spiritual nature. If our feelings are directed by passion, idle fancies and vain imaginings, we will fall into our lower nature or self, which is capable of oppression.

Prior to my talk, I had learned from Mitsuko Yamamoto that the Japanese people are afraid of "cults", so I was careful in my presentation, speaking of 'Abdu'l-Bahá as a great educator. As it was, the turn out for my presentation broke all records even though the rule is "don't let outsiders in." The Principal, Mr. Kow was impressed with my resume, found support with the president of the PTA and was able to pull it off with record attendance.

I was supposed to speak for 1 hour, but felt I had said all I could say in 45 minutes, so opened it up to questions. Naoko was astonished that they asked questions so openly, that it was a very rare occasion. The talk was audio taped and Naoko transcribed it. It will be attached to this report, as will be my presentation in China. Another result is that Naoko has been asked to give my Protective Behaviors for Children Program to this Elementary school at some time in the next two months. And the representatives of the other 3 elementary schools have asked her to give the "Importance of Feelings" program at their respective schools. The teachers and parents, once they heard snippets of what I taught in China, begged me to stay one more day and teach the "Protective Behaviors for Children."

But I had an appointment the next day. It was beautiful that this "closed society" was slowly opening its doors. Here is the workshop I presented for them.

Importance of the Development of a Feeling Language In Children and Adults
You can find handouts for this program at my website:
www.skylarkpubl.com

The program that I have chosen today is to teach you about children's feelings. But for you to understand children's feelings, you have to understand your own feelings. You'll find a blank piece of paper in your file. Draw a line in the middle of it from top to bottom. Write down a feeling word on the left side for what you feel right now about being so busy about coming down to this program.

(Pause and give them time to do so.)

On the right side, write down all the feeling words you can think of in 3 minutes. Don't worry, this is just for you. You won't have to show it to anyone else.

(Pause for 3 minutes to give them time to do so.)

Count the feeling words. I always take only 2 minutes for this in the US and the highest number I've ever gotten is 25. How many had 15 or more? **(Wait for show of hands.)** How many had 18 or more? **(Wait for show of hands.)** How many had 20? **(Wait for show of hands.)** In order to teach children and nurture them, we need to know "feeling language" which is very difficult if it hasn't been taught or allowed. The next thing I want to do is to hand out the list of feeling words. There are over 250 words for feelings in English. Yet we have troubles expressing our feelings.

When I was a little girl, and I tried to express my feeling, my mother hit me in the mouth. And my mouth bled. My father beat me with the belt when he was angry. And I had red marks all over my legs. I could not cry. But I was hit if I was happy, too. Things were very mixed up in my family life. So I learned not to express my feelings at all. This was very confusing to me. When I grew up, all I did was rage. I raged at my sewing machine, when it didn't work right. I raged at my dog. I raged at my children and I am very ashamed of that. But the only feeling I had was rage. So I had to learn from the beginning how to express all of my feelings.

(Hand out the paper with the feeling words in English)
If you'd look at this piece of paper, you'll see many feelings that there are. There are even more feeling words than that, that we don't have words for.

Here is what it sounds like to make a sentence that describes how you feel when you are upset or even when you feel happy. "I feel _____ when you call me names because then I think you don't like me." OR "I feel _____ when you ask me what I think because then I know you think I am your equal."

Pick out three feeling words on the list that describes how you have felt during the past week and make feeling statements about them to the person sitting next to you. They don't have to be revealing statements. They can just be everyday common feelings. Nothing private or secretive that would embarrass you.

(*Give them 10 minutes to do this assignment.*)

Now, I'd like to hand out another piece of paper with all the faces that show feelings. Do you recognize some of these facial expressions? Do some of them make you laugh? Have you ever seen any of these expressions on the faces of your children or friends? You don't have to fill out all the blanks under the faces right now. It's a tool you can use with your own children.

(*Hand out the paper with the faces that show feelings.*)

You can point to a face and ask your child or student, "Do you recognize that feeling? What is that little boy feeling? How does the little boy or girl feel?" It can help you recognize your own feelings as a parent, too.

When I was 34 yrs. Old, I felt like a failure as a parent because of my rage. So I took a course of parenting. It was 6 weeks long, one night a week. I recommend a course in parenting to every parent, every grandparent and every teacher in this room to take these courses at least once in your life time. One night we spent 2 hours talking about feelings. It was like they were talking a strange language to me. I couldn't identify my feelings at all. I had written a story in 1973 about a little bird who learned to fly. It was a story of my life as a little girl. I didn't know what to do with it after I had written it so I hid it in my drawer. But after I went home from the parenting course, I took out that story and I read it again. 'Skylark' is the name of my story. Skylark is the bird who couldn't fly. When I read it again, I saw that Skylark did not express his feelings of being abused. So I had written 15 pages with no feeling words in it. I had described people, plot, events, and story, but my characters didn't use any feeling words. All I could do was an intellectual exercise. I wrote in the feelings that Skylark would be expected to feel. But I still could not feel my feelings. I didn't know it, but this was a major turning point in my life because I began to notice the times that I wasn't allowing my children to express their own feelings. This was in 1976.

To be able to share your feelings with another human being, you would have to be able to trust them. I did not trust others with my feelings because I had been abused when I tried to share them and, also, because my father sexually abused me when I was 2 through 8 years old. I kept this a secret from my first husband in 9 years of marriage, and I kept it a secret from the man who was to become my second husband. Secrets like that destroy trust.

Fortunately, six months after we were married, we attended a weekend "Marriage Encounter" program during which we were to write out our feelings 3 times a day for 20 minutes and then discuss them privately. I felt compelled to trust my husband and tell my secret. I had thought that no one would want me if they knew, but I overcame that fear and wrote him a letter, pouring out my heart and my secret to him. Then I waited while he read it.

What would his response be? Would he turn away from me? Would he not think me worthy to be his wife? None of that happened. He said, "Now I understand why you wrote your Skylark story and present it to groups and organizations. I didn't understand before but now it fits." I was 39 years old and I had finally told someone my secret. But my feelings were still blocked, locked up, and ice cold.

It took me until I was 46 yrs. old to express my feelings.
Those extra feelings all of the rage of feelings were
connected to my telling the secret of sexual abuse when I
was a child. Until I would tell the secret in a support group
and have the injustice validated, all those feelings were
blocked. And I had to grow up from a little girl who
couldn't express feelings or identify them to an adult who
could.

One of the goals of parenting is to teach children to identify
and name their feelings. 15 yrs. old is about the age of
maturity. By 15, 16, 17 yrs. old, a child should be able to
express their feelings and identify them. But that's not the
final goal. The final goal is that when the child becomes an
adult, all those feelings must be governed and regulated by
love, compassion, and virtues. Love, compassion, and
virtues should be an umbrella over all those feelings.
Because feelings are like energy in our body. They cause
us to have a biological, psychological experience. That
energy has to be expressed in appropriate ways. Running,
jumping, sports, talking, sometimes I have to hit a pillow.
When I got angry at work, I would go into the bathroom,
and run in place. One day I raged at my boss. After 8 yrs.
of working for him, I raged at him. Then I yelled "I'M

GOING HOME, NOW." And he said, "Are you coming back tomorrow?" I said, "YES!" Then I went home and couldn't eat. I couldn't sleep. I worried all night long because I had to go back to work tomorrow morning. The very next morning, I was entering the radio station I worked at like a scared puppy, and he was waiting right there for me. I walked up to him and said, "I am sorry I got mad at you yesterday." He said, "You have nothing to apologize, for you were just expressing your feelings." He understood.

And the next week, a man came to be interviewed on a live program about a book he had written, called "All the rage". He was going to give a seminar that weekend on anger. I decided to take his seminar. I studied anger from different sources for 7 yrs. And I began to teach Anger Management at the college. I stopped raging at my children.

How young can you tell to teach children about feelings? At what age? I can give you an example, a story about my sister. She and her 2 1/2 yrs. old daughter were visiting us for Christmas. All the adults were gathered together in the living room talking. And my niece, Natalie came running into the room screaming. My sister put her arms around Natalie. She said, "Tell mama, I'm frightened of the helicopter." My sister was teaching my 2 1/2 year old toddler niece about feeling language. And my little niece said, "I'm frightened, Mommy." And another time, I saw my sister looked at my 2 1/2 yrs. old niece and said, "You look sad, are you?" And this little girl could affirm that. My sister then had the opportunity to ask my niece, "What are you sad about? What has happened?"

This is teaching children to identify feelings. There is a story of Belinda. I was sitting at a table at the Bahá'í World Congress, a conference in N.Y. A woman was telling a story of her daughter who was 6 years old. Her daughter's name was Belinda. The mother was away at an evening event and a babysitter was taking care of Belinda. When she came home, the babysitter was left, he was a man. But it could just as well have been a woman. And Belinda said, "I hope Derrick doesn't ever touch me where he did again." And the mother's heart began to beat very fast. "Where did he touch you?" She said, "Right here," pointing to her pubic area. "How do you feel?" she said. She keyed in the feeling words immediately. Belinda at 6 years old could tell her mother, "I feel Yucky." "Do you want to talk about it?"

"No, I just want to go to bed", she said. "Well, we'll put you to bed, but if you want to talk about it in the future, I have a special friend who would love to talk about this with you."

The point is Belinda was allowed and invited to express her feelings. She had been taught to express her feelings. I don't know how 'yucky' translates into Japanese, but it can translate into 'disgusting'. Now Belinda is a grown up woman about 19, 20 years old and she is healthy, because she was allowed and encouraged to express her feelings at 6 years old and the situation was not buried. These are just 2 examples of teaching children to identify and express their feelings. Those who are aware of feelings and have not buried the shame of abuse or fear of bullying can heal faster.

A great educator named 'Abdu'l-Bahá was once asked, "What is the purpose of life?" He said, "The purpose of life is to develop the virtues." My message today is not only to encourage children to share their feelings, but to encourage them to learn the virtues at the same time. One virtue that I have had to learn is 'forgiveness'. At some point in my journey of healing, I learned to forgive my mother and father. Remember earlier I said that the goal of childhood is to identify all the feelings. Then the goal after 15, 16, 17 years old is to have love, compassion, and virtues to be umbrella over all those feelings. Because feelings are just feelings, they just tell us about what is going on inside of us. They do not determine our behavior. And choices must be made based on virtues. We have much to learn from who had been abused. People who had been abused have difficulties with the virtue of 'trust'. They have difficulties with 'forgiveness'. But they can teach us much about the virtue called 'detachment'. Detachment can lead us to purity of motive. Detachment can lead us to peace. Detachment can lead us to understanding of our behavior and choosing behavior, and can lead to world peace. I believe that the suffering people of the world can teach us much about peace. If you look at the list of feelings, you'll see some of them seem to be negative. Some of them might be feelings that bullies have. The reason they are there, is so that we will learn that human beings have two natures. We have a spiritual nature. And we have a physical nature. The feeling that you see that might be negative, might be expressed by our physical nature. That is why we need the virtues. If we are compassionate, we may not be indignant when someone injures our feelings. If we look into ourselves, we would know that we have the same feelings that any other human being has. Our great educator and philosopher said, "All the people of the world are one." Many educators have said to be kind to your enemy. So I'm going to end this program this afternoon with thanking you for coming. I think I've run out of things to say. So if you have any question, I'll take questions now. I'll think immediately of things to say. Thank you.

Question: When my child showed his/her anger, I said to him/her why he/she is so mad at such a simple thing. Eventually he/she ended up with that he/she doesn't want to talk about it anymore. I think there might be a boundary of a child as a human being, and no one is not allowed to invade it without his/her permission. How do you think about it?

Answer: If a child shows his/her anger, please ask him/her, "Are you mad? You seem to be mad, are you?" And say, "Sometimes mom gets mad, too. Let's show angry faces together." I've created some children songs. I'll sing one of them for you.

"Let your inside feeling match your outside face. So you don't become invisible. Learn to share your feelings when you really get mad, and you won't feel so terrible. It's a sad, sad feeling to be all alone. When you need a hug, but your heart's a stone. So tell a friend what's deep inside. It's Ok if you want to cry. (Name) you can't hide, so let your feeling show outside."

Let them know that it's not the anger that is bad. It's the behavior. I know 18 yrs. old boy was so angry that he put his fist through the wall and made a hole in it. The anger wasn't wrong. But he needs it to have an opportunity to express without his mother getting mad at him. He needs to express it in appropriate ways. Don't be afraid of anger. Face the fire. Face the dragon. So you can encourage them to regulate it.

Question: I sometimes feel guilty or incapable as a parent…

Answer: You need to develop forgiveness for yourself as a parent. We are taught in many cultures to blame ourselves for whatever goes wrong. Women are the first educators of children. So therefore, they feel that they are doing everything wrong. They don't usually have enough support. But you are doing a good job. We blame ourselves and we allow others to blame us. Would you forgive your best friend? Would you forgive your child? If you can, then you can forgive yourself. Parents need support. That is why you are bound together as parents and teachers. The answer isn't blame. The answer is tools and powers. I blamed myself for 15 yrs. and finally I went to a parenting course. My mind exploded with new ideas. Then I went home to try to use it. My 12 year old boy said, "Oh, mommy, you just learned that out of a book." And I did. There is a woman's poster that I created. I want to tell you about.

"If a woman pursues her good against all odds, Under the harsh gaze of all those she loves, All those who love her, all those who don't care for her, Even those who don't know her... Giving them their right to judge her every moment, Every memory, every mistake on the way... And still find a way to love herself, Take responsibility for her growth, And continue pursuing her good, and the greater good, She will find that her NOBILITY is a light that radiates from within, not from without! I have this and I wish it for you." (Phyllis K. Peterson, 1991) When I wrote that, I had the courage to stand up to the judgments of anybody. I stand up to the judgment of my parents. I stand up to the judgment of my brothers and sisters. I stand up to the judgment of my adult children. If I didn't, I wouldn't be gone from my husband for 2 weeks. I'm a tough lady! (laughter)

Question: Recently I am trying to conquer or overcome anger. I used to show my feeling only by my behavior, but I realized that it makes much easier if I use words openly express my feelings. For example: When I am tired, I didn't tell it to my children but act like I am tired. Now I tell them that I am tired and without telling any further my children began to help me. Don't you think it has related to your talk?

Answer: Yes, it does have a strong relationship to what I said. Mothers and Fathers can't put themselves upon pedestals. My mother never said, "I'm tired." Consequently, I worked till I hurt my body. I didn't know I was tired. It is healthy to tell children what you are feeling. It's not healthy, however, to lean on children emotionally. It's not healthy for the Mama to tell children, "I'm depressed." We have friends for that. Relatives, husbands, sisters and brothers can help, too. Children are too young and tender hearted to deal with such problems. They don't have the emotional resources to deal with such problems. They are naturally empathetic. Emotions are not to be repressed. They are not to be controlled. They are simply to be regulated. Do you see the difference between that? We always have different feeling impulses. They give us information about ourselves.

If a 10 year old boy, like the woman said, is expected to control his/her anger 24 hrs. a day, he would eventually explode. When I exploded at my boss, I was fortunate that he understood feelings. If a 10 year old boy exploded in the school compound, it's a different story. So children need outlets for anger.

Question: How do you think about the social factors that cause more of those abuse cases to happen?

Answer: The world is gaining greater awareness. These things have been going on for decades in secret. In the USA, one out of 4 girls is sexually abused. One out of 7 boys are molested before they are 16 or 18. In South Africa, in the report of the cases of child sexual abuse, 33% of it is done by the school teachers. In India, 25% of population has been sexually abused before the age of 16.

There is child sexual slavery in India and Thailand. (There are similar reports on other countries, too.) In Brazil, a child is sexually abused in every 30 minutes. It is a worldwide epidemic. The reason that I give you the statistics is to tell you that though I'm not a healer, I teach people prevention. I have another program that teaches prevention. Sharing feelings is an integral part of prevention. So it addresses the social problems. We can't be a world society or world global society of people who do not express their feelings. What do you see around the world right now is but rage and war. Look at the youth who rioted in France last year. Look at the fact, that there are 400,000 cases of bullying reported each year in a so called civilized country like Great Britain. These are angry children. So I implore you as parents and teachers to teach your children to express their feelings openly.

Question: Do you think have there been these cases before and just recently does it reveal its reality owe to the IT development?

Answer: It has been there before. The world is going through a moral crisis right now. Each school, each family and each community has to address the moral issues of the days in which we live. We can't live in a moral free society. And we can't be morally neutral. That is why I travel and teach. I could stay home and just watch TV. I taught in China last year where I spoke at the UNESCO conference and presented a program called Protective Behaviors for Children. And I stayed 5 extra days, so I can teach teachers and principals the Protective Behaviors in the class room setting. I hear Japan has a wonderful program that they have implemented called CAP (Child Abuse Prevention). Australia is the leader in child abuse prevention.

Question: I am teaching the 6th grade, 41 children. The list of virtues is very useful. But I am struggling teaching children morals because they can't catch the meaning of virtues. They are just joking around and can't take it seriously. It seems chaos to me. Do you have any suggestion for this?

Answer: There is a wonderful book called "Family virtues guide". Please refer to: http://www.virtuesproject.com for more information. Treating virtues as a joke happens in America, too. This virtues project has exercises, games, and projects. It can guide the teachers in the way of teaching virtues in many ways. What I don't know how to do is to deal with behavior problems. Parents, teachers, and communities, all have to work together. Parents are taught to be educated in virtues and demonstrate them at home. The teacher has to be educated in virtues and demonstrate patience, forgiveness and firmness. The small community needs to be informed, so that parents work together and teachers work together with the children. As far as children losing their interest, I know that children today have very short attention spans. And the media affects the children's attention span. I'm not blaming the media, but everything like feelings has to be regulated and to be moderated. If a child watches TV 4, 5 hrs. a day, they don't get a chance to express their feelings. They are like Zombies. Parents watch TV 4 hrs. a day, they are like Zombies, too. They miss opportunities to have family intimacy. And it's so hard when there are so many children.

Question: We have children from Elementary and Junior High schools in our community. There are some children who have troubles within their hearts. They tend to exclude other children and tell lies. But I don't want to label the children as bad children. I prefer to treat them as equal.

How should I treat these children? Do you know any best ways?

Answer: Tough question. I repeat. The world is going through the moral crisis right now. Our job is to show kindness to everyone. And show compassion and love to everyone. Are you worried about protecting your own children? (No…) I pray for people that I am worried about. And I teach whatever corner of the world I find myself in. I can't heal bullies. I'm here to teach you about feelings, prevention of bullies. I wish I could heal bullies. There are a lot of bullies in the world I would like to heal. The world is going through a moral crisis. And my part is the prevention and teaching about feelings and virtues. And virtues can help. Virtues must be taught simultaneously with feelings because of our dual nature…a physical nature and a spiritual nature. Reach the children you can and trust in a higher reality. Thank you.

Note: Excerpts from "Assisting the Traumatized Soul" and "Healing the Wounded Soul" used by permission of the National Spiritual Assembly of the Baha'is of the United States of America.

Friday, November 11th: This morning I go by train to Kyoto for the Peace as a Global Language Conference at North Kyoto University. I was met at the train station by Pioneer to Japan, Marilyn Higgins. Since we both arrived around 11:30 AM and the Conference didn't start until evening, we took our luggage and personal items to our little Japanese Inn and then went sightseeing to the Golden Pavilion[12], built by an emperor several centuries ago as a place of relaxation and pleasure. The landscaping was lovely with brilliant red fall leaves dotting through the gardens.

Saturday, November 12th: Marilyn and I sat in on several sessions on topics such as Domestic Violence, How can NGO's get the Media's Attention, the rebuilding of Cambodia, NGO's in Pakistan conducting earthquake assistance as well as promotion of equality of women and men. We had opportunities to chat with Marilyn's former contacts as well as make new contacts, one of which,

---

[12] **Kinkaku-ji** (金閣寺?, literally "Temple of the Golden Pavilion"), officially named **Rokuon-ji** (鹿苑寺?, literally "Deer Garden Temple"), is a Zen Buddhist temple in Kyoto, Japan.[2] It is one of the most popular buildings in Japan, attracting a large number of visitors annually.[3] It is designated as a National Special Historic Site and a National Special Landscape, and it is one of 17 locations making up the Historic Monuments of Ancient Kyoto which are World Heritage Sites.

Professor Craig Smith, Kyoto University of Foreign Studies, wants to create an event and bring me back to Japan. Dr. Smith was one of the plenary speakers of the Conference.

Sunday, November 13th: We attended the closing sessions in the morning and then took the train south to Yamaguchi in the afternoon, where Marilyn's husband, Michael, met us and drove us to their home. Their adult children were there with the grandchildren and Michael fixed dinner for all of us. I went to bed exhausted and drained of all energy at 9 PM, not knowing if I would be able to attend to my responsibilities of three meetings the next day.

Monday, November 14th: 10 AM Mitsuko Yamamoto arrived with 3 women and we had an hour and a half consultation with Mitsuko as the interpreter. I discovered that I had met one of the women on a previous trip to Japan (2002) when she was hospitalized for 1 ½ years. She wept when she realized that I had remembered her and had prayed for her even though she had no memory of the incident.

Another group arrived at noon for a luncheon and a second consultation. One of the women fell into my arms sobbing as soon as the door opened. She cried in my lap for 25 minutes. No one had to translate; I knew she was a survivor of sexual abuse.

Marilyn and Michael worked all day at the university while I prepared for a Fireside that evening. They had a student house guest and had invited him to the Fireside. I told stories of Women and Girls as Heroes, tying them in with the quote of 'Abdu'l-Bahá: "Unless women are allowed to attain their highest possibilities, men will be unable to achieve the greatness that might be theirs."

Tuesday, November 15th: I headed north by train for Shinagawa, where Naoko Kagami met me and guided me back to Fujisawa. This was a 4 ½ hour trip which could have been disastrous had I not purchased a Japan Rail Pass in the U.S., good for 7 days. A tiresome journey, but I rode in comfort in reserved seating.

Wednesday, November 16th: One quick meeting with the ladies who represented the other 3 elementary schools. They wanted consultation with me about personal problems and wanted to connect with Naoko about future plans for her teaching in their schools. They have decided to become a support group for one another now.

At 11 AM I boarded the train from Fujisawa for Narita…the Narita Express, no changes, straight through to the Airport! Hooray! Divine Assistance every step of the way!

My flight left at 5:50 PM and I slept all the way home.

My plane arrived at 2:15 PM at O'Hare International Airport on Wednesday, November 16th, and my husband, dear soul, met me at the airport so I didn't have to wait for a bus and endure a 2 hour bus ride home.

Follow-up e-mails!

-----Original Message-----
From:
To: _____
Cc: Skylarkpp@aol.com
Sent: Tue, 29 Nov 2005 21:31:53 +0800
Subject: You will love this A.

Dear _____,

I know you are looking for some good and appropriate education and teachers to help you provide loving, virtues based classes to the children in your neighborhood in _____ And you know I want to help however I can.

One way would be to offer this workshop attached. I just finally read over the entire workshop last night and I am so moved. I shared it with a friend today on the university campus I live on in Beijing and we're going to see if we can't offer the workshop to our English corner group of education master's degree majors. We talked about consulting with our group about the possibility of sharing with the Psychology department. Then consulting about the possibility of getting more information about how the local authorities handle abuse issues and then find a way to offer the workshop to the community on a regular basis. People don't know how to talk about this here in China either, but this workshop makes it so much easier to talk about what needs to be talked about.

Please see the attached information and read it over at least once or twice. This workshop can be done in about 45 -60 minutes I think. And it can be fun for kids and adults. It's so necessary and easy, too. It's called "Protective Behaviors for Children". If you have any questions please call on me or on Phyllis Peterson who wrote the workshop and presented it here in Beijing last month at an international conference on education. She and her husband live in IL and I've cc'd Phyllis (Hi Phyllis, are you home now from your travels?).

With lots of love,

_____

-----Original Message-----

From: skylarkpp@aol.com [mailto:skylarkpp@aol.com]

Sent: Wednesday, November 30, 2005 3:31 AM

To: _____

Cc: _____

Subject: (Rising's prompt - This mail may be a junk mail)Re: You will love this _____

Dearest ,

Thank you so much for doing this!!! This is wonderful! Yes, the program can be done in 45 to 60 minutes. After the conference was over I stayed on for five extra days and presented it in full to S.Y., H.S. teachers (she has 7 kindergartens), and Mr. L. teacher's, and D. V. of the Daystar Academy. So I had the opportunity to influence the teachers of approximately 3,000 plus students, and some parents who were present.

Then I went on to Japan where I spoke to approximately 75 people who were representing 4 different elementary schools. Which was very unusual because outsiders are not allowed such a privilege. All was well, however, and these people were hungry for knowledge and the question and answer period took up a full 45 minutes.

I spoke on the topic of "The Importance of the Development of Feelings in Children". The workshop and handouts are translated into English and Japanese and the English has already been transcribed by someone who took dictation from the audio tape that they made. I am attaching the workshop and the handouts for you to see if you can use them. If you have someone to translate this into Chinese, it would be wonderful. If not, perhaps someone who speaks English could read it to a group, while a Chinese interpreter could do the simultaneous translation for the group. As you will see from the handouts, I already have it in English/Japanese.

My appreciation for what you have done and what you are doing.

And all my love,

Phyllis

Dear Phyllis,

Thank you so much for your email and encouragement. I'm so glad your trip to China and Japan was so successful and helpful. Thank you for the materials from your Japan trip – wonderful. My friend, a graduate student here at Beijing Normal University has offered to translate the feeling document into Chinese and I will send you a copy as soon as I can. I was wondering if we could put these documents that you've sent including your paper and handout from the ESD forum, on a website for others to download? I could not find them on your site: http://www.skylarkpubl.com/. Perhaps we can use it as a reference to help folks give the workshop in their communities? I'm really inspired to use both your workshop materials and also the Virtues Cards in work with kids I do here in China and also to share with other friends and educators. I'm considering taking a teaching job here at the university and will hopefully be able to work more with the teachers. I'm very excited and will report back to you what I do here in China.

With lots of love and thanks to you,

P.S. I'm reading the part about the 7 Valley now in your newest book. Love it so much.

Dearest _____,

RE: "My friend, a graduate student here at Beijing Normal University has offered to translate the feeling document into Chinese and I will send you a copy as soon as I can. I was wondering if we could put these documents that you've sent including your paper and handout from the ESD forum, on a website for others to download?"

Of course, you may have her translate the feeling document into Chinese and make a website for both documents. I have been polishing the "Feeling" document and don't know if you have the updated version so I will attach it to this e-mail with the extra handouts. I, too, am excited about the possibilities of your proposal and look forward to receiving a copy of it in Chinese, and the website.

Also, please keep in touch and let me know if I can be of any assistance to you!

All my love, dear soul, Phyllis

Dear Friends,

My quiet times I spent in prayer.

My busy times were like a prayer.

And my tired times were spent in gratitude for this wonderful opportunity.

That my husband could share this with me fills my heart with joy. I also feel a deep connection with all the troubled souls that I met on this trip. I welcomed them with open arms and not once did I feel burdened by their stories. They shared like sisters and I listened like a sister.

I will attach my programs that I presented. Hopefully, you will be able to make sense of all of it.

With loving regards and deepest gratitude for your prayers while I was in China,

Phyllis K. Peterson

Dear Phyllis,

I'm so glad you wrote – I wanted to congratulate you on your new book and the wonderful promotion that is going on in many bookstores. I'm thrilled to know a famous Bahá'í author! Your report was excellent and I've filed it, with many cross references to make the information accessible. I think you have made a tremendous impact on those you met in China. You have done that very well. I hope you continue to travel to China and keep us informed about your work there. And I encourage you to carefully plan your trips so you won't get too exhausted. I'm speaking from experience, as you well know.

Loving regards,

Ruthie Gammons

2007:

I went back to China on November 12, 2007. My Mother passed away while I was on the plane. I gave my workshop at the UNESCO Conference, then I had to return home prematurely for her funeral.

PART THREE

SWAZILAND

Phyllis K. Peterson and Nancy Good

September 7th through October 5th, 2006

For several years I was a member of a list serve on
Education on line, where I wrote about my teaching trip to
Thailand and Japan. Irma Allen from Swaziland responded
to my e-mails, asking me if I would be willing to come to
Swaziland and teach the children, parents, and teachers
about "Protective Behaviors for Children", as I did in
Thailand. She said they would not be able to pay for my
transportation, but would take care of all of the rest of the
necessities. I jumped at this opportunity and soon
Botswana would be added to the trip.

I did my homework for this trip and discovered that the
HIV/AIDS infection rate was at 42% for both of these
counties and that men thought they could be cured of
infection if they had sex with a virgin child. My concern

was great and their desire to combat this disease was even greater.[13]

My itinerary was wall to wall for this trip and I had no time to journal about my daily activities. My ground crew was amazing. My amazing daughter, Nancy Good, came with me and was an excellent assistant. We arranged to meet in O'Hare, she coming from Nashville and myself coming from Rockford. We were thrilled to have each other's company.

September 7[th, Thursday]: Departure from O'Hare

September 8th, Friday: Arrival and 8 hour layover in London

September 9[th, Saturday]: Arrival in Johannesburg then on to Swaziland, picked up by Dale Allen at 10:30 AM

September 10[th,] Sunday: Bahá'í School at the National Bahá'í Center

---

[13] This infection rate for Botswana is now 23% (in 2016). Swaziland remains the highest in the world.

September 11th, Monday:

Assembly for Forms 1 through 4 (equivalent to High School): 200 Youth

Boundary Sculpting Game: You can find handouts for this program at my website: www.skylarkpubl.com

The Boundary Sculpting game, is a game which takes one through unconscious feelings and responses to boundary violations that shows one is in stress to concrete steps one can take, such as making the violator aware of one's feelings and needs and asking (ideally) for acknowledgement and reciprocity. One cannot develop true unity and cooperation with others or obedience to authority unless their identity and boundaries are also protected. The game starts with an unwanted hug from a friend, co-worker, or relative. There are 9 sequences of Boundary Violations to go through.

Empowerment of Women was also presented. You can find handouts for each of my workshops at my website: www.skylarkpubl.com

Empowerment Workshop

There are many ways to empower women and men. I have chosen to dismantle a series of negative messages and awaken men and women to affirmations that confront this covert insidious, destructive language that causes despair, anxiety, helplessness, hopelessness and unnecessary rebellion. Instead, I have imbued the following positive messages and higher thinking affirmations with the powers of "Authority of Self," using the "thought, feeling, action model to rise above the negativity.

Identifying the Negative Messages and Oppressive Language:

Don't be smart or intelligent! Don't ask questions! Don't be close! Don't be weak! Don't be strong! Don't need! Don't be a child! Don't learn and grow! Don't lead! Don't be happy! Don't see from your perspective! Don't be important! Don't be afraid! Don't change! Don't laugh! Don't be different! Don't set boundaries! Don't be aware! Don't be sane! Don't trust! Don't be you! Don't try! Don't talk or express yourself! Don't know yourself! Don't be! Don't take care of yourself! Don't be greedy! Don't make choices! Don't disobey or challenge authority!

This language is in direct opposition to encouraging us to use our birthright powers... the power of speech, the power of choice, the power of discernment, the power of identity, the power of wisdom, the power of intuition, the power of reflection, discovery, faith, and understanding....the power of will, memory and to search for truth....the power of response, anticipation, attention, and receptivity....and the power of reasoning, deduction, and to recognize a Higher, Superior Being.

Sometimes the language that imprisons our powers is directed as "You are lazy! You are stupid! You're crazy! You're BAD! You made me hit you! You are worthless! You're retarded! You whore!" No matter how the language is framed, the fundamental relationship is that of disempowerment of authority of self and destruction of our identity. These are "Labels" that we internalize; and we believe them to be true. But if we have someone, a friend, parent, therapist, or support group, that reflects our good qualities (which should have been done while we were children through adults) instead of receiving a negative label, we begin to believe in ourselves and our true identity becomes strongly resistant to external criticism or even victim to pathological self-criticism. Further, we begin to know how to "affirm" our good qualities which the following exercises will illustrate.[14]

In "The Girl Within," Jane Hancock explores the lives of 20 women raised in a patriarchal system. She discovered there are many excellent virtues which were **trained out of the women when they reached the stage of adolescence.** It was acceptable for the girls to have these virtues at ages 8 through 10 years old, but many of the virtues would not fit into a patriarchal society as the girls turned into women. Sounds familiar, doesn't it? There is a quotation in Stanley Milgram's book, "Obedience to Authority:" "Behaviors that did not enhance the chances of survival were successively bred out of the organism." How ironic that today we must reacquire these behaviors in order to survive. To continue, in the adolescent stage the limited traditional roles the women were to be forced into were carefully delineated and any "independent" virtues and "authority of self" they had developed up to that point, were carefully weeded out.

Each of the 20 adult women had reached a point where they were unable to meet life's challenges because they were

---

[14] Dr. David Burns, "Feeling Good: 10 Cognitive Distortions that can cause depression.

thwarted by their own submissive adaptation to the roles that were assigned to them. It was only when they reached back into their memories to reawaken the vibrance of the 8 to 10 year old girl within, whose "authority" had been exorcised by patriarchy that they integrated the strong virtues that were theirs originally. They were then able to resolve the problems that had previously seemed insurmountable. When this occurred at age 32, 47, 58, or 72, they felt complete, whole,...."authority of self" re-established. They were no longer disempowered.

Feelings:

Feelings are very important to this exercise because if we have been disempowered, our feelings are going to be negative. This can result in depression and/or a loss of a feeling of nobility. Our thoughts are going to be negative, too, and they, together, will negate our ability to act to change our behavior. There is much research that has been done on how to change how our brain thinks. In "Liberating Greatness: The Whole Brain Guide to An Extraordinary Life", authors Hal Williamson and Sharon Eakes say that an "affirmation when tagged with emotions create strong, new neural circuits" in the brain. "These new circuits have the capacity to alter old, unwanted behaviors in favor of new, desired behaviors"[15] because they lift us up out of the despair, paving the way for new thoughts which enhance our esteem and nobility.

Right now, think of the happiest moment you've ever experienced in your life! It may be a moment when you have achieved or accomplished a goal, the birth of a baby, the feeling you had when you learned to drive and became more independent; when someone saw the real you and accepted you. At any rate, it is an "I can do it!" moment that brought you great joy! Bring up the memory of it, then bring up the "Feeling" you had. What Mr. Williamson suggests is that you take that special, positive feeling and tag, connect, mark, or attach it to your new affirmation. This will create the strong neural circuits that will help you alter your old, unwanted behaviors and emotions. Whatever challenge you are experiencing needs to be tagged emotionally with that joyous feeling, instead of the feelings of disempowerment that weigh you down. When the negative thoughts repeatedly come up, as they always have, use the following affirmations and tag them with the invincible feeling of joy! Doing it repeatedly will actually change your brain given time! Repeat the affirmation

[15] Hal Williamson and Sharon Eakes, Liberating Greatness", copyright 2006, Word Association Publishers, Pennsylvania, p. 197

"identically" three times, or craft your own affirmation, but remember to tag it with a positive emotion while you do so!

There are actually "twin concepts" to adopt to win the battle: Tag the affirmation with the positive emotion; and "detach" your mind and heart from the negative emotion. Becoming detached actually opens you up to a myriad of positive and wonderful emotions.

An Example of the Affirmations and Acknowledgements:

1. Don't be smart or intelligent! You're stupid!

Q. What feelings and thoughts about yourself would prevent you from revealing that you are smart or intelligent?

Partner #1: (Look directly and with compassion into your partner's eyes for one minute before you speak. It's more to stop people from being superficial, to make them pause a moment to contemplate the need inherent in another.): I acknowledge that you are an intelligent person. You don't have to pretend to be stupid with men, women, or authority. I encourage you to develop the power of independent investigation of truth today. You can discover a new reality with your power of reasoning, and feel joy while you do so!"

Partner #2: (Look directly and with acceptance and trust into your partner's eyes for one minute before you speak): I challenge the belief that I have to pretend to be stupid with men, women, or authority. Today I will look for ways to reveal instead of conceal my intelligence. I will develop the power of independent investigation of truth. I will discover a new reality with my power of reasoning by bringing my inner thoughts into public view. I will speak my truth without fear. I celebrate my visible intelligence. I tag this affirmation, these new thoughts, with a feeling of joy that comes from a memory of a prior accomplishment! And I repeat this affirmation word for word, knowing it will lead to a change in my behavior! (Feel the joy you remember and then say the affirmation three times with that feeling of joy glued into every word!)

This first acknowledgement and affirmation is followed by 28 more that are connected to the negative messages at the beginning of this workshop which can be found at my website.

September 12th: Tuesday

Grade #1: Protective Behaviors for Children - 8:30 to 9:30 AM - 60 children

Grade #2: Protective Behaviors for Children - 9:30 to 10:30 AM – 60 children

Grade #3: Protective Behaviors for Children - 11:15 to 12:15 PM – 65 children

Grade #4: Protective Behaviors for Children - 12:15 to 13:15 PM – 68 children

Protective Behaviors for Children Outline
You can find handouts and coloring sheets for this program at my
website: www.skylarkpubl.com

1. Opening: What you will learn:
    a. How to ask for help

b. Who to ask for help

c. How to conquer your fears

d. How to say "No!"

2. Describe the three kinds of touch: Gentle, hurting, and secret touch. Use a doll or stuffed animal to demonstrate. Pat the stuffed toy or baby doll gently to show how we must treat children. Tell them that is gentle touch. Ask the children if they've ever been pinched or hit. Tell them that is Hurting touch.

3. Secret touch is done to your private places. Where are your private places? (some children will know.) Anywhere you can cross your arms on your body. No one is allowed to do hurting touch or secret touch there. What about the Doctor or someone who is trying to do good for you?

a. Give them pictures #1 through #4.

b. Face – Have them cross their arms over their face. Talk about the feelings the boy is showing on his face in picture #1. Write them down in the blank spaces. The child can write the feelings in their own language.

    c. Chest – Cross arms over their chest. Talk about the feelings the little girl in picture #2 is showing on her face. Write the feelings down.

    d. Pelvic area or genitals. – Cross arms over their pelvis. Talk about the feelings the boy is showing in the picture #3. Write them down.

    e. Buttocks – Cross arms over their buttocks. Talk about the feelings in picture # 4.

4. Demonstrate the song: "This is my private place!" Then have them stand up and sing it three times.

This is my private place (cross hands over face).

This is my private place (cross hands over chest.)

This is my private place (cross hands over pelvis.)

ONE! (face)

TWO! (Chest)

THREE! (Pelvis)

AND (Turn around)

FOUR! (Slap your backside on four)

5. Hand out the markers or crayons. Now let them color the pictures. Encourage them and review as you walk around the tables. Say things such as:

What a good job you are doing.

I like the way you color.

Can you tell what feelings are in his or her heart by the expression on the face?

You have a special way of coloring.

What's your favorite color?

Do you like to color at home and at school?

6. Tell me what it's like when you feel embarrassed or ashamed or Yuckie or disgusted. (Pause and wait for answers. Acknowledge their embarrassment.) If you feel ashamed when someone does secret touch, it's not because of something you did but because of what the other person did. They should feel ashamed.

7. Hand out the picture of the hand and the pencils. Have them write "NO!" "STOP!" and "HELP!" in large letters in the palm of the hand. Tell them that the hand is a universal symbol for "NO! STOP! And HELP. Have them yell "NO!" as a group as loud as they can! (Tell them that wasn't loud enough and tell them to yell "NO!" again. They'll get the idea and you will have a better result.) Do the same with "STOP! And "HELP!" Have safe scissors ready.

8. To stop hurting touch and secret touch, you have to be able to tell someone who is safe, someone you can trust, someone who would only do something good for you and to you. Who is safe? Start with the thumb and write in a name of someone who is safe. Raise your hand and tell me who is safe! (You'll get a variety of answers. Write them on the board.) Mom, Dad, Auntie, Grandma, brother, cousin, friend, Doctor, Policeman, Nurse, Teacher, Counselor, Principal, Uncle, Grandpa. Write one of these names on each finger and thumb. Cut out the hand.

9. Tell the person on the thumb. If the person on the thumb doesn't listen, tell the pointer finger. If that person doesn't listen, tell the next, and keep telling until someone listens. Don't stop! Be brave!

10. Color the hand red, which Is also a universal symbol for stop. And cut out the hand. Have everyone raise their red hand in the air and on cue yell, "NO! STOP! HELP!"

11. Closing: What have we learned today? Ask them to raise their hands and   say what they have learned.

    a. AND, tell them, "Nothing that can happen to you is so terrible that you can't say it out loud to someone you trust!" Say it again, "Nothing that can happen to you is so terrible that you can't say it out loud to someone you trust."

SONG: This is my Private Place! (Sing it three times.)

Thank the children and parents for coming today! If this class has been conducted in a school room, they can put all the hands on the bulletin board as a reminder of what they have learned and the teacher can review the points.

NGO – SOS[16] – 2:30 PM

Ruhi Class with Fireside at 7 PM at Baha'i Center

September 13th: Wednesday

Pre-School: 8:30 – 9:30 AM – 75 children –

Protective Behaviors

---

[16] SOS Children's Villages in Swaziland

The work of SOS Children's Villages in Swaziland started in the 1980s. An agreement was signed between the organisation and the Kingdom of Swaziland, and the national SOS Children's Villages association was founded in 1987.

In mid-2000, SOS Children's Villages launched an SOS Emergency Relief Programme to help the numerous families affected by heavy floods in the vicinity of Mbabane. In 2002, persistent droughts and food shortages affected the entire country. Again, an SOS Emergency Relief Programme was set up and many families were provided with food and medical assistance.

Due to increasing rates of HIV/AIDS, the organisation decided to implement an SOS Family Strengthening Programme, aiming to enable children who are at risk of losing the care of their family to grow up within a caring family environment.

At present, SOS Children's Villages is supporting Swazi children and young people in three different locations by providing day care and medical assistance. Children whose families cannot take care of them can find a loving home in one of the SOS families.

Grade #5: Protective Behaviors for Children – 9:30 – 10:30 AM – 62 Children

Grade #6: Protective Behaviors for Children – 11:15 – 12:15 PM – 67 Children

Grade #7: Protective Behaviors for Children – 12:15 – 13:15 PM – 69 Children

September 14th: Thursday

NGO- SWAGAA (Swaziland Action Group Against Abuse)– 9:00 – 10:30 AM

Form #1: Chastity and Abstinence – 11:30 to 12 Noon – 35 Youth

Form #1: Chastity and Abstinence – 12:00 – 1:30 PM – 27 Youth

Form #1: Chastity and Abstinence – 1:30 – 3 PM – 38 Youth

I created several vignettes for discussion regarding chastity to teach the youth. They are as follows:

Vignettes for Discussion on Issues of Chastity

Separate into four groups to discuss these vignettes. [Or make it a group discussion if the numbers are small.] Appoint a secretary to take notes on your observations, insights, and conclusions. When we gather after the discussion, the representative of each group will report the findings. These stories are meant to give you a variety of perspectives from different cultures around the world, so you will know you are not alone when facing issues of Chastity.

1. Sharnaz, 14, has been raised to follow the Qur'an and by Western standards has had a very strict upbringing. When she was 9 years old, the entire family moved to the U.S. The airline flight posed difficulties when a particularly questionable movie was shown that her parents thought was extremely inappropriate even for adults. Sharnaz and her siblings, male and female, had to wear scarves over their eyes to protect them from the evil of the sexual content and language in the movie. They do not have a TV in their home. Here she is living in the U.S. with all the freedom that surrounds her and she is beginning to doubt her religious teachings and feel rebellious. What are the moral dangers her parents are trying to protect her from? She is feeling isolated because she has no one to talk to about her internal turmoil. How does she gain a voice

and learn how to make responsible choices based on her religious upbringing?

2. Mark is 15 years old. His father, though successful in his career, is an alcoholic and uncommunicative as well as a womanizer with multiple sexual partners. Mark's father has infected his mother with HIV-AIDS. His mother is passive and doesn't believe she could make it on her own if she left her husband. Besides, she would be beaten, an outcast from her family and lose her children. She was raised to be submissive. Complicating things is the fact that Mark is stimulated biologically through a romantic relationship with a young classmate. They have progressed from romantic feelings to romantic behavior and she is pushing him to go further. He wants desperately to have someone he can communicate with but he doesn't have a moral model at home to guide him. Mark is alone, not being parented. This vacancy in life can leave him lonely and vulnerable. Many young people are turning to each other in personal relationships which are intended to be substitutes for and an alternative to bonded relationships with family, friends and community. How does Mark develop the ability to be intimate with others and remain chaste? Since he doesn't have a moral model through the

influence of his father, how does he create one? How can a loving community help him? If you were in this situation, who would you talk to?

3. Sha-Rhonda is 16 years old. She has been raised in a solid family unit where there has been open communication throughout her childhood during which her voice has been encouraged and responsible choices have also been encouraged. She has watched her parents negotiate their needs with one another, and they have taught her how to negotiate her needs. This has been modeled for her all of her life. She has learned to both separate herself from the world, yet to be open to it, kind of like Jesus saying, "Be ye in the world, but not of the world." She, too, experiences romantic feelings and biological stimulation from time to time, but does not engage in romantic behavior. She wants to be chaste until she marries and then absolutely faithful within marriage. She has an evolving moral motivation, with the support of her family and community that steers her toward true intimacy in relationships as she works toward completing her education and providing service to her community.

She also reads the Writings of Baha'u'llah and monitors her thoughts and behavior in order to strive toward absolute chastity on a daily basis. She knows that attaining ANY virtue absolutely must be her goal, regardless what her peers are doing. But we must always keep in mind that we must strive with spiritual energy for the highest standard possible regarding chastity. What is evolving moral motivation as compared with absolute chastity? Some youth will make mistakes but should know there is forgiveness and God is Merciful. Absolute chastity is the Baha'i standard we should strive for outside of marriage and our youth should be encouraged to maintain that aim, whether that involves ones thoughts and actions or the use of drugs or alcohol and the way one speaks in an elevated manner to others. What will support Sha-Rhonda's morality as she matures? Even she is in danger if she is not taught how to make decisions about her sexuality. What are the components of Shoghi Effendi's definition of chastity she will have to negotiate?[17] What will happen when she experiences powerful biological stimulation? What

---

[17] See the listing of the different components of chastity from "Advent of Divine Justice," pp. 181-182 ahead in this book.

will help her keep her mind on the goal? What is the goal? What is your goal?

4. Perry is 21 years old and in his 2nd year of University. He is not interested in having a long term relationship and wants only a "friend with the benefits of sex." He has two part-time jobs that he has to juggle, papers to write, research to do, classes to attend. He has no time for the traditional standard of dating. It takes too long. He doesn't want to complicate his life with emotions. He just wants sex with a friend, yet he is depressed all the time and doesn't know why. Statistics on people who subscribe to "friends with sexual benefits" and have multiple partners shows that 2/3rds are depressed because of their experiences. Why do you think that is? What do you really want in a healthy relationship? Perry would just move on if a woman wanted to negotiate boundaries in their relationship. Could you set boundaries or negotiate your needs with Perry? Is this a one-sided relationship? If it's one-sided, who has all the

power in this relationship? Do you know someone like Perry?

5. Layli was sexually abused and exploited at the age of 12 by an Uncle. She then went into prostitution by the time she was 15. Abuse by her uncle, led to lack of sexual boundaries and self-depreciation for Layli. Many young women like Layli are unprotected, are not within an active family system, and their community life has disintegrated...there is no one to protect and guide them. Layli has feelings of being unworthy and being damaged for life. Outwardly she laughs at the idea of chastity, but inwardly she longs to lift herself up out of this promiscuous behavior. Does she blame her Uncle? Or does she become responsible for her choices? Can she make choices in the culture and social context in which she lives? Or is her early powerlessness going to be played out all throughout her life? How can she unite with a loving, supportive community when she is afraid of being judged? How can obedience to a Higher Authority help her moral motivation to evolve so that she can attain and maintain chastity? Is

chastity a one-time-only opportunity for us or are we always assisted to return to it by a loving, merciful, bountiful God? What are your thoughts?

6. Meeko had to drop out of school and is unemployed. She wants someone to love her; someone she can have intimacy with. An older man asked her to go out with him and she jumped at the opportunity. He infected her with HIV/AIDS and she is now pregnant. She wants to protect the baby within her womb and realizes that she should not take another lover. Relationships with older men are so very common among young women who have few resources and no defined future options. In the absence of hope for something better, they seek an imagined protector with some material resources because it looks like a good choice that comes with security. What are Meeko's choices now? What are her chances for survival? Where can she turn for help, education and knowledge in her community thereby increasing her options? If God is Merciful, how does this happen to such an innocent, gentle person like Meeko who wouldn't hurt anyone? Meeko discovered that globally, over

3 million children are estimated to be living with HIV/AIDS. Many of these babies were infected either before birth, during labour, or through breastfeeding. She also realized that since she should not breast feed her baby, she would be stigmatized by many in her culture who would frown upon bottle feeding. Should she tell someone at the Natal Clinic in order to protect her child? If you knew ahead of time that dropping out of school and dating an older man would put you at risk for HIV-AIDS, what would your decision be? (a) Abstinence until marriage, (b) seeking open communication to negotiate your sexuality, or (c) risking your future and that of your children? Would you fear being abused? If so, what resources would you seek out in the community in which you live? Do you know someone that all of this has happened to? You don't have to name any names, but can you tell something about their struggles.

7. Back in the mid 80's I was working for a company. My boss was sexually harassing me. It started when I was an unmarried woman and I was flattered by the attention. But then I married my husband; and I became very uncomfortable by this behavior. I kept

resisting and he kept persisting. By not stopping it I was actually passively participating. I kept praying that he would stop, but there was a power there. There was a biological power, a psychological power, an emotional power and there was lust. Again, I kept resisting and telling him "No!", but he would continue. I told my husband what I was going through and he said, "Can't you just tell him no?" That was not working. I was afraid of losing my job and I had three children to support. I couldn't avoid his advances. But I kept praying. In the midst of all this, Baha'u'llah brought a Baha'i to my workplace. I had been inactive in the Faith for ten years. Just his presence was an answer to my prayers. I continued to pray, became active in the Faith again and realized that I had to become brave enough to tell him a NO with finality without any worry about the outcome. For some reason I remembered a quote of Baha'u'llah's from Gleanings where He wrote: " Say: Set ye aside My love, and commit what grieveth Mine heart?"

(Baha'u'llah, Gleanings from the Writings of Baha'u'llah, p. 307)

It was such gentle, impassioned plea and rebuke that I made my decision. I waited till closing time. Everyone had left the building. I went into his office and told him that he was not to harass me anymore. It was over. I did so and I believe I achieved absolute chastity at that moment! However, up till that moment my morality was evolving, through knowledge, through reading the writings, through prayer. I could not achieve absolute chastity without it being preceded by an evolving morality. My boss went on to have an open relationship with his secretary, even kissing her on the mouth in public, whereas he kept ours a secret. I never reported my indiscretion or his to anyone, though he was abusing his power as an authority figure. Looking back, it all started with an "innocent" hug. A friend asked me the following questions after I sent this to her:

Is it freeing to tell this story? Is it releasing shame?

Has self-contempt hounded you for having enjoyed the attention?

Is there redemption in the strength that comes from facing temptation and listening to God's making a way of escape?

Are you experiencing the freedom of forgiving yourself?

Can you look the people in the eye who expected perfection without blemish, knowing that their expectation of perfection throughout their lives was impossible for them to achieve, and they all have a story to tell.

Here's what the Baha'i Writings have to say about Hugging between unmarried men and women:

"The pilgrim's note reports the Master as saying: 'Women and men must not embrace each other when not married, or not about to be married. They must not kiss each other... If they wish to greet each other, or comfort each other, they may take each other by the hand.' In a letter to an individual written on behalf of Shoghi Effendi it is said: 'The Master's words to... which you quoted, can certainly be taken as the true spirit of the teachings on the subject of sex. We must strive to achieve this exalted standard.' (October 19, 1974)

(From a letter of the Universal of Justice to the National Spiritual Assembly of the United States, February 10, 1974)

(Compilations, Lights of Guidance, p. 439)

Response from the Guardian to John. B. Cornell

Oct. 19, 1947

Dear Baha'i Brother:

Your letter dated Sept. 21st has been received and our beloved Guardian has instructed me to answer it on his behalf.

What Baha'u'llah means by chastity certainly does not include the kissing that goes on in modern society. It is detrimental to the morals of young people, and often leads them to go too far, or arouses appetites which they cannot perhaps at the time satisfy legitimately through marriage, and the suppression of which is a strain on them. The Baha'i standard is very high, more particularly when compared with the thoroughly rotten morals of the present world. But this standard of ours will produce healthier, happier, nobler people, and induce stabler marriages. The Master's words to Ann Boylan, which you quoted, can certainly be taken as the true spirit of the teachings on the subject of sex. We must strive to achieve this exalted standard.

Assuring you of his loving prayers for the success of your Baha'i services.[18]

With warm greetings,

R. Rabbani

P.S. If the N.S.A. wish to publish this in Baha'i News he has no objection.

May the Beloved bless your efforts, guide your steps, and enable you to promote the best interests of His Faith,

Your true brother

Shoghi [Effendi]

A Chaste and Holy Life: Such a chaste and holy life, with its implications of modesty, purity, temperance, decency, and clean-mindedness, involves no less than the exercise of moderation in all that pertains to dress, language, amusements, and all artistic and literary avocations. It demands daily vigilance in the control of

---

[18] The letter from the Guardian to Cornell may be cited to the Ocean database, "Ann Boylan Pilgrim Notes." It should also be mentioned there that most of that letter is also reprinted in *Lights of Guidance*, section 1210.

one's carnal desires and corrupt inclinations. It calls for the abandonment of a frivolous conduct, with its excessive attachment to trivial and often misdirected pleasures. It requires total abstinence from all alcoholic drinks, from opium, and from similar habit-forming drugs. It condemns the prostitution of art and of literature, the practices of nudism and of companionate marriage, infidelity in marital relationships, and all manner of promiscuity, of easy familiarity, and of sexual vices. It can tolerate no compromise with the theories, the standards, the habits, and the excesses of a decadent age. Nay rather it seeks to demonstrate, through the dynamic force of its example, the pernicious character of such theories, the falsity of such standards, the hollowness of such claims, the perversity of such habits, and the sacrilegious character of such excesses.

(Shoghi Effendi, The Advent of Divine Justice, p. 28)

Dinner Party at Dale Allen's Home:
Presented: "Authority of Self": 7 PM

Definition of Authority of Self

I define "Authority of Self" as: the freedom and ability to use birth-right mental powers to make rational and moral choices, self-regulation of the emotions; and the right or permission to act independently with the understanding that one has personal limitations.[19]

Mankind is in need of new powers and virtues, new moralities, new capacities in the day in which we live. They are fully within our grasp....such as the power of speech, the power of choice, the power of discernment, the power of identity, the power of wisdom, the power of intuition, the power of reflection, discovery, and understanding....the power of will, faith, memory and to search for truth....the power of response, anticipation, attention, and receptivity....and the power of reasoning and deduction.

September 15th: Friday

Montessori Pre-school and Kindergarten: Protective Behaviors – 65 Children

9:00 – 10:30 AM

NGO – SOS – Workshop on Anger Management for Orphan children and Staff

---

[19] Phyllis Peterson, Assisting the Traumatized Soul

Left Mbabane at 4 PM for Kruger National Park in South Africa. Dale Allen was our guide and arranged this trip specifically for my daughter, Nancy.

September 16th: Saturday
    Kruger National Park with Dale Allen, Nancy Good, Phyllis Peterson, Ali Javid,
      Kathryn.

September 17th: Sunday
    Kruger National Park in South Africa

September 18th: Monday
    Form #2: Chastity and Abstinence – 8:00 – 9:30 AM – 25 Youth
    Form #2: Chastity and Abstinence – 9:30 – 11:00 AM – 20 Youth
    Form #2: Chastity and Abstinence – 11:00 to 12:30 PM – 32 Youth
    Form #2: Chastity and Abstinence – 12:30 to 2:00 PM – 21 Youth

    NGO – Orphanage – 3:00 PM

Community Gathering – Storytelling – The Heroic Female Spirit – 7 PM

"The Legend of the Guardians of the Forest," "The Girl Who Climbed a Ladder to the Stars."

After I told these stories a woman approached me and said, "Shame on you! Where is your DVD? Our people don't want to read stories in books; they want to see and hear storytellers! Where are your DVD's??" I had to admit I did not have any and I was ashamed.

September 19th: Tuesday

Form #3: Chastity and Abstinence – 9:50 – 10:30 AM – 20 Youth

Form #3: Chastity and Abstinence – 10:30 – 11:15 AM – 32 Youth

Form #3: Chastity and Abstinence – 11:30 – 1:00 PM – 35 Youth

Ruhi Class and Fireside

September 20: Wednesday

Form #4: Chastity and Abstinence – 8:00 – 9:15 AM – 36 Youth

Form #4: Chastity and Abstinence – 9:15 – 10:30 AM – 28 Youth

Form #4: Chastity and Abstinence – 10:30 – 11:30 AM – 26 Youth

Dinner with Performance at Nuri's home – 6:00 PM – 9:00 PM

September 21: Thursday

NGO Meeting for SWAGAA – Training the Trainers Program:

Protective Behaviors for Children

The Importance of the Development of a Feeling Language

Public Meeting 7 – 9 PM at the Omni Conference Center – Training the Trainers Program on Protective Behaviors for Children – over 50 people in attendance.

PART FOUR
September 22 through October 5, 2006
Botswana

September 22nd: Friday

Departure for Botswana, Picked up by Phillip Huebsch at 5:20 PM. An official at airport arrival looked at my passport and wanted to know where I was staying. I had been trying to get through to my Botswana contact without success and could not answer because I did not know. I felt helpless. The official would not return my passport; told me to go outside and see if anyone was waiting for me. I did so and Philip Huebsch told me to tell the official that I would be staying at the Bahá'í Center. I returned to the airport and informed the official and he said, "Oh, Bahá'í!!" and immediately stamped my passport. When I returned to Philip, he informed me that the Government of Botswana mandates that 5 religions be taught in Botswana: Christianity, Islam, Buddhism, Hindu, and Bahá'í. They teach all these religions in the schools and universities.

September 23rd: Saturday

3 – 6:00 PM – Women's Gathering at Meena Sabet's home

Telling my Story of recovery from incest and trauma through the Revelation of Bahá'u'lláh, based on my first book, "Assisting the Traumatized Soul."

September 24: Sunday Two children's classes at two of the Baha'i Centers

Ind. Avenue at 8:30 AM – Protective Behaviors for Children

Broadway: 10:00 AM – Protective Behaviors for Children

Lunch with Billy & Christine Lee

Block 9 Youth – Chastity and Abstinence – 5:00 PM

September 25th: Monday – 8:30 AM – 12:00 Noon

Workshops with 33 Primary School Teachers

On Boundary Sculpting and

Anger Management

2:30 PM – Meeting with 30 student peer counselors at Mogoditshane

CJSS – Training the Trainers on Protective Behaviors

7:00 PM – Gave a Fireside at Rosa's

September 26th: Tuesday

Meeting with teachers at Matlala – 8 – 8:30 AM – BOCONGO[20]

Meeting at Emang Basadi with Members of NGO's 9 AM – 12 Noon

Training the Trainers on Protective Behaviors

Tshedisa Institute[21] – 4 to 6 PM – Ava and Thato

Telling my story of recovery from trauma through the Revelation of Baha'u'llah.

7 PM – Nineteen Day Feast

September 27th: Wednesday

---

[20] The Botswana Council of Non-Governmental Organisations (BOCONGO) is the national umbrella body for non-governmental organizations in Botswana. BOCONGO was officially registered in 1995 with the registrar of Societies (Registration Vision A strong, vibrant and accountable NGO Status. Mission To facilitate the strengthening of Local NGOs for effective participation in the development process of Botswana.

[21] The Tshedisa Institute offers innovative strategies in medicine, wellness, creative arts therapy, psychological services and HIV/AIDS treatment, prevention and care. It is a centre where health care providers, as well as the community can safely address the physical, emotional and spiritual needs.

Rainbow Primary School – Training the Trainers in Protective Behaviors

(Headmaster Mr. DeGraaff) 10:00 – 11:00 AM

Meeting with the teachers of Secondary Schools of the Ministry of Education:

Training the Trainers in Protective Behaviors – 2 – 4 PM at the Bahá'í Center, then Anger Management and Feelings. (related to passion killing.)

September 28th: Thursday

Radio Program with Rolene Sher at 12:15 – 1 PM

Motivational Speech to Encourage Success with Exams at end of October for

200 students of Form 3 at Matlala CJSS

September 29th: Friday

Rainbow Secondary School – 9:20 – 10 AM – Forms 1 and 2 – 70 female students

Chastity and Abstinence

10:30 to 11:10 AM – Forms 3 and 4 – 75 female students – Chastity and Abstinence.

Couples Gathering at Dr. Roya Sham's - 6:00 PM

The Boundary Sculpting Game and Criticism Story

September 30th: Saturday - A DAY OFF!!! (Well, almost!)

Afternoon with Representatives of two NGO's during which I did

Storytelling: The Heroic Female Spirit, 3:00 – 6:30 PM

October 1st: Sunday

Meeting with youth and children in Block Nine – 9:30 – 11:00 AM

Storytelling: The Heroic Female Spirit

Community Gathering at the Tlokweng Baha'i Center – 6:00 PM

Storytelling: The Heroic Female Spirit

October 2nd: Monday

Private Consultation: With Joal. Meena, my hostess, was very concerned that I was going out to dinner with Joal and I did not understand why. She wanted a private consultation, which we had at a hotel restaurant.

But when we left the hotel and got out into the parking lot, men were approaching Joel's car. She told me to get in the car immediately and lock the doors. Then I understood Meena's concern and wished that I had invited Joel to meet with me in my upstairs bedroom. I have a lot to learn about safety in a foreign country.

7 PM – 25 Baha'i Youth – Chastity and Abstinence Workshop at Rosa's

October 3rd: Tuesday

Meeting with the staff of Gaborone City Council, a group of 33 Social Workers

8:30 till 12 Noon.

Training the Trainers in Protective Behaviors for Children

The Importance of the Development of a Feeling Language in Children and Adults

In these last few days, I was to present to the Gaborone City Council in Botswana; and I was puzzled about this; I couldn't realize a connection between the City Council and my mission to prevent child abuse. When 33 people arrived, I could tell they did not want to be there; and they had a difficult time settling in. But by the time 3 ½ hours had passed in these "training the trainers" workshops, such a mood had been created that none of them wanted to leave. Then a man stood up and began repeating almost word for word what I had said in my 2 workshops that I had presented; then he revealed that he was the director of the 33 social workers who were a branch of the Gaborone City Council and that he intended to take the two workshops to every quadrant of the city. I could tell that he was very capable and very sincere.

What transformed the group of 33 social workers? I sang songs of "Let your inside feelings match your outside face," "Is this a safe place? I'm looking for a safe place where I can share my feelings. A place where my child within can feel her anger and express it", and "I'm listening to you, woman. Thanks for speaking from your heart. I heard you share your feelings. Wish you'd done it from the start." Then I proceeded to tell them that hidden feelings of resentment unexpressed and unacknowledged can lead to the rage that fuels the passion killing they see in their country. Hidden feelings and the threat contained in women becoming equal with men are also blocking the emancipation of women in South Africa. By then, as the workshop progressed, their hearts began to melt and the questions began to flow until no one wanted to leave. The following are the songs I wrote and sang to the counselors who are branch members of the Gaborone City Council and also to the youth of the high schools:

BE REAL AND FEEL

Be real and feel
Don't hide inside
Reveal what's in your
Heart and speak what's on your mind.

Begin within,
Then let it out
Don't worry how
It sounds,
Just let the feelings out.

You won't feel bad
Because you're being real
You hurt inside because
You cannot feel.

Be real and feel
Don't hide inside
Your friends won't turn away when they can
See the real you.

INSIDE FEELINGS/OUTSIDE FACE

Let your inside feelings
Match your outside face.
So you don't become
Invisible.

Learn to share your feelings
When you get real mad
And you won't feel
So Terrible.

It's a sad, sad feeling
When you're all alone.
And you need a hug
But your hearts a stone.

So tell a friend what's
Deep inside.
It's OK if you want
To cry.

Louis Timothy
You can't hide!
So let your feelings
Show out side.

IS THIS A SAFE PLACE?

Is this a safe place?
I'm looking for a safe place
Where I can share
My feelings

A place where my child within can
Feel his anger and be respected
If I feel safe, I'll let you come close.
If I feel safe, I won't hide
I have the power to share or withdraw
Give me some space, and my feelings will thaw.

Safety is essential
But I need boundaries
Instead of walls
Show me that you will respect all my rights.
I'm setting boundaries. They're clearly in sight.

Is this a safe place?
I blossom in a safe place
Where I can show you
Who I am!

THE LISTENING SONG

I'm listening to you woman,
Thanks for speaking from your heart.
I heard you share your feelings,
Wish you'd done it from the start.

You were scared to tell me
But you did it and I'm proud.
I know you trust me with your real self,
Cause you're not invisible now.

I'm gonna' listen to all my friends.
I'm gonna' hear their feelings when they're mad
Cause we can work it out if we talk.
If we share our feelings, we won't feel bad.

I don't want to lose my good feelings of myself.
So I'm gonna choose to show you my real self.
I'm mad, I'm sad, I feel so very bad.

If we want to have a happy day,
We'll listen to each other as we play
Too many feelings can be quite a load.
If we share them quick
We won't EX - PLODE!!!!!!

Motivational Speech for the Women of Matlala –
1:30 – 3 PM

Tshedisa Institute – 4 – 6 PM – Boundary Sculpting Game (w/Ava & Thato)

October 4th: Wednesday

11:30 AM – Private Consultation with Otsile

2:00 – 4 PM – Student Teachers at Molepolole College of Education

Training the Trainers in Protective Behaviors

Anger Management in the Country of Botswana where people show no anger, (we are not an angry people) but there is a lot of "passion killing". In one newspaper account of a passion killing, a woman was let off if she did not kill anyone in the next 5 years.

October 5th: Thursday

Departure for Johannesburg, London, and O'Hare.

Follow up E-Mails

Hello Phyllis

Thank you for your email, the publications and most of all thank you for your time and sharing your story. Your presence and contribution at SWAGAA made a lot of difference. Staff felt motivated and the information could not have come at a better time than this when we are reviewing our training manuals so that they focus more on prevention and awareness creation.

Regards

_____

_____

SWAGAA Director

Swaziland

"Some people are always grumbling because roses have thorns and I am grateful that thorns have roses"

****

One 7 year old girl, who was leaving the class and not addressing anyone, was heard to say, "I LOVE this class!"

The next day a 1st Grader popped into my class to say, "I told my mother and father about what you taught me yesterday and they said I was to do exactly what you said."

Ten minutes later another 1st Grade boy stopped by to report, "I shared what I learned in your class with my father and he told me he wanted me to continue learning more about this."

These are indicators that parents are truly concerned about the HIV-AIDS crisis in Swaziland, which has the highest percentage rate (42%) in the world.

After I gave an initial Fireside on a Monday, the Bahá'í youth who heard that I was going to teach "Chastity and Abstinence" for the High School students were begging me to return the following Monday to give them a workshop on "Chastity and Abstinence." Some of them were infected with HIV/AIDS. The rest of them wanted knowledge for protection against it.

The youth at the Rainbow Secondary School in Botswana, owned privately by a Baha'i couple, dubbed me a "Modern Day Mary Poppins" because I was addressing the issues they face on a daily basis and doing it through music and storytelling.

When I gave my final program to the public in Swaziland, a Bahá'í woman in charge of an NGO introduced me to the gathering. After I finished speaking, she noted that in 1997 they had had a Conference on Prevention of Child Abuse and HIV-AIDS issues, but had only come up with "recommendations". Then she added that I had come with "practical applications" that are vital to put into action...but I had come 10 years too late for those who were lost to HIV-AIDS.

Dear Phyllis
Thanks for the e mail and your continued trip of mercy, which I am sure will change the future for many who will take the advice and apply the one two three and four etc.

At the base of this serious hiv aids pandemic is a corrupt
abuse of children practiced by a decaying society in want of
values and ethics and the spirit of God as renewed by
Bahá'u'lláh.
The Baha'i School is a growing seed bed for these ideals
and values to take root and grow and spread.
We thank you for your efforts made in behalf of
Bahá'u'lláh.
Yours will be the greatest of rewards - not in this world.
We look forward to your return anytime.
Much Love from Irma and I.

Dale Allen, Allen Bahá'í School in Mbabane, Swaziland

The purpose of my trip to Swaziland and Botswana was
to show the connection between the issues they are facing
right now re: HIV-AIDS and what Baha'u'llah's Revelation
has to say about the moral dangers that are
currently blocking a solution for Africa and
other continents. "Protective Behaviors for Children" is a
one hour workshop for Pre-K through 6th grade, using art
and music to teach about boundaries for young children, the
powers they have, and how to ask for help. Child sexual
abuse is rampant in South Africa; and Botswana and

Swaziland have the highest percentage of HIV-AIDS (42%) in the world. Men also believe that if they have sex with a virgin child, they will become free of HIV-AIDS. Incest and rape is epidemic.

The empowerment of women and conflict resolution are high on the list of needs.

From: skylarkpp@aol.com
To: _____
Sent: Sunday, October 22, 2006 1:52 PM
Subject: My itinerary in Africa

Dear _____,

Attached is my itinerary in Africa. They said I raised prevention, awareness and discussion to a new level. I came prepared, but the Friends in Swaziland and Botswana carefully coordinated and choreographed my trip, even my meals, so that it would be a success. They had firm contacts and made appointments in every level of education, governmental, non-governmental organizations, and social. I am so grateful to them and to my home community for their prayers which kept me going.

When they said I came ten years too late for the loved ones they had lost, my heart sank. But they also said I brought hope with the practical application that they so desperately needed. Who is to tell if I have brought a false hope or a concrete plan that if applied with follow-up on a regular basis, has created a structure for the future? I don't know, George, but if God allowed me to go, perhaps there are reasons beyond my capacity to understand. I do know that Africa has a special place in my heart and that I will go back.

Love, Phyllis

(Reply From George Davis, Assistant for Protection then, but on the Regional Council today.)

Dear Phyllis,

What a blessed privilege to serve and to know that what you have offered has been of great benefit to others. We are also blessed to live in a time when the resources and capacities of the world wide Bahá'í community are increasingly able to support our individual efforts to minister to the crying needs of humanity even though the task is impossible to fully achieve at this time. Your ability to have the impact you had on your recent trip is in many ways the result of the capacity of the Bahá'í community to support your efforts in addition to your own individual initiative. Ten years ago that capacity was more limited. And so our ability to serve effectively as individuals is intimately connected with the capacity of our community to channel and support individual initiative. In this way our collective influence as a leavening force on humanity at all levels is magnified. Even so we are unable to fully evaluate the long range benefits or affects of our efforts.

I am reminded of the following statement of the beloved Guardian of our Faith:

"With the age that is still unborn, with its herculean tasks and unsuspected glories, we need not concern ourselves at present. It is to the fierce struggle, the imperious duties, the distinctive contributions which the present generation of Bahá'ís are summoned to undertake and render that I feel we should, at this hour, direct our immediate and anxious attention. Though powerless to avert the impending contest

the followers of Bahá'u'lláh can, by the spirit they evince and the efforts they exert help to circumscribe its range, shorten its duration, allay its hardships, proclaim its salutary consequences, and demonstrate its necessary and vital role in the shaping of human destiny. Theirs is the duty to hold, aloft and undimmed, the torch of Divine guidance, as the shades of night descend upon, and ultimately envelop the entire human race...The field, in all its vastness and fertility, is wide open and near at hand. The harvest is ripe. The hour is over-due. The signal has been given. The spiritual forces, mysteriously released, are already operating with increasing momentum, unchallenged and unchecked. Victory, speedy and unquestioned, is assured to whosoever will arise and respond..."
(Shoghi Effendi, Messages to America, p. 28)

May your love and services to the people of Africa continue to bear fruit.

Loving Regards Always,

_____

Dear Phyllis,

Allah'u'Abhá

How are you? We are still feeling the impact of your visit. The lady from "life Line" who has attended your workshop at Emang Basadi is very interested to push your workshop " protective behaviouor " to all the children under 9 in Botswana. she promised she will try to coordinate among the ministry of education, Gaborone city council and all the revelant NGO and the Bahá'ís. We are still waiting to hear from her.

_____, the guy from Gaborone city is always busy, I manage to spoke to him only once after you left. He was out of the town. Now he is very busy with some other projects, he will not be in his office for the rest for the month. We have a plan to visit him to give him the folder.

His email address:

I am really enjoying your books. It is very educational and open another horizon for me to examine the Baha'i writing.

Take care

with Bahá'í Greeting,

_____

Dearest _____,

Please send me your physical address so that I can send you
the music audio cassette tape that goes with the "Feelings"
program. _____ wanted to have the music
lyrics, which I left with Meena, but I also want to send the
music on tape for _____ and the NGO's to use. I will send
15 to 20 for you to divide amongst them. OK? I love the
Gaborone LSA for all they are doing to push this forward.
Please keep in contact. I would be willing to come back to
Gaborone to do two weeks of "training the trainers"
programs to kick this off. Tell everyone!

Love, Phyllis

Dear Friends, (sent out to over 100 NGO's of several countries in Africa)

I recently returned from a trip to Swaziland and Botswana, where I presented 65 programs in 25 days to children, youth, women, teachers, school counselors, social workers, principals, orphanages, NGO's and others on "Protective Behaviors for Children: Prevention of Exploitation", "Boundaries: How can they protect me from HIV-AIDS?", "Authority of Self: Empowerment of Women", "The Importance of the Development of a Feeling Language in Children and Adults", and storytelling re: "The Heroic Female Spirit: A Collection of Tales."

My schedule/itinerary is attached. Pictures of my presentations can be seen at my website below. Click on Photographs at the bottom. If you are interested in the "Protective Behaviors for Children Program", I am attaching it for free, *with the hope that you can use it and would pass it on to other NGO's that work with women and children.* It is a one hour program to be presented to children, with handouts to color and cut out. There is also a "training the trainer" program attached regarding my own story of recovery from incest from the age of 2 through 8 years old.

I am also the author of "Assisting the Traumatized Soul" (1999), "Healing the Wounded Soul"(2005), and "The Heroic Female Spirit: A Collection of Tales" (2006), published by the Bahá'í Publishing Trust. Also, "Remaining Faithful: Meditations on Being True to Yourself, Your Relationships and Your Principles," (A Compilation, Published by Special Ideas in Indiana); "Seeking Intimacy in a Diverse Community: Seeking the Spiritual Reality of the Mentally Ill, the Physically Challenged and the Emotionally Wounded" (published by George Ronald in England); "The Universal Theory of Man: Authority of Self" and "The Skylark Life Skills Manual for Women and Girls," (Published by Skylark Publishing Co.)

I am told by _____ in Gaborone that there is a woman who saw my presentation at Emang Basadi who is interested in spreading "Protective Behaviors for Children" to all children 9 and under throughout Botswana in a coordinated effort with other NGO's, the Ministry of

Education and the Gaborone City Council 33 member Social Workers. Please have her contact me if she needs my assistance in anyway. I would be willing to return to Botswana to do "Training the Trainers" programs. I am at your service.

Thank you for your interest.

Phyllis K. Peterson

-----Original Message-----
From: _____
To: skylarkpp@aol.com
Sent: Mon, 27 Nov 2006 3:23 AM
Subject: Re: Protective Behaviors for Children

Hey Phyllis
Thank you so much for all the material you sent us. LifeLine Botswana is very interested in carrying out this program for the children because from our monthly statistics, it is evident that more and more children are being sexually abused and I am sure many cases go unreported.

Attached is a profile of LifeLine Botswana, so that you understand the organisation better.

We shall be getting in touch with you for technical advise and whatever else we might need.

Thanks for the support and for allowing us to use your knowledge to reach out to children and empower them.
Regards

_____

Dear _____,

Attached is another program that I have developed. I don't know if you were the woman who sat in on my class at Emang Basadi, but this one was also presented that day. I am truly grateful to be in a position to help in any way that I can. Just let me know when and where.

"The Importance of the Development of a Feeling Language in Children and Adults" was, by the end of my presentations with the Gaborone City Council (_____ and his 33 social workers), tied in with "passion killing"....and anger management. You may already have some of this material because of the work you do.

Also, I have created a game called "The Boundary Sculpting Game" which I could bring or send which slows down the process of recognizing exactly what interpersonal skills are lacking or present, making the unconscious process conscious, in setting boundaries. Let me know if you want me to bring copies of the game or send them. I am sincere in wanting to come if you need me.

Thanks for sending me the attachment on Life Line local, national and international. It is very impressive.

All my appreciation for the work you are doing.

Phyllis

(From _____, Director of 33 Social Workers branch of Gaborone (Botswana) City Council.)

Hi Mrs Peterson!

Thank you very much for the documents, i will really make utmost use of them. I hope to communicate with you in future. Have a happy christmas and prosperious new year. May God bless you and your family.

Thank you very much!

skylarkpp@aol.com wrote:

Dear _____,

Here is the attachment for the Workshop on "The Importance of the Development of a Feeling Language in Children and Adults", plus "Protective Behaviors for Children: Prevention of Exploitation", two "training the trainers" programs, complete with handouts. Thank you for your interest and your dedication to the children and families of the city of Gaborone.

Warm appreciation, Phyllis

PART FIVE

Botswana

April 9th – 17th, 2007

I left the United States with high hopes for the planned
conference of "training the trainers" in "Protective
Behaviors for Children" in Gaborone, Botswana, Africa.
As my plane flew over Chicago, the pilot said we would be
flying between Chicago and Milwaukee. I looked out the
window to my right and there in perfect position was the
Bahá'í House of Worship, as if confirming the mercy
mission that I was on.

I can't possibly express the gratitude and privilege I feel
because of this opportunity that keeps growing as word
spreads about the program I have developed that can
contribute to the moral development of children and the
education of their parents. The need is so great, and the
women of Africa are so dedicated and desperate to meet
that need. I taught them that an aware child is a protected
child.

Because the problem of HIV/AIDS is multi-faceted, no one
program will be found to resolve it. My program is
actually a six part program and still won't meet all the

needs such as food insecurities and shelter insecurities, human trafficking, rape as well as changing cultural traditions that are ingrained in the minds and hearts..

- "Protective Behaviors for Children: Prevention of Exploitation
- "The Importance of the Development of a Feeling Language in Children and Adults
- "The Authority of Self Workshop: Empowerment of Women"
- Obedience, Chastity and Abstinence"
- "The Heroic Female Spirit: Storytelling"
- "Empowering our Daughters."

I arrived in Gaborone on Wednesday, April 11th, 10:30 AM. _____ picked me up and brought me to her house. I slept until 4 PM and shook off my jet-lag. Tahboho, a young woman brought me to Lifeline Botswana for the three day conference, which started at 9:00AM on Thursday, April 12th through Saturday, April 14th.

_____, Director of Lifeline Botswana, had brought together her counselors, other relevant NGO's, therapists, and parents. I gave a three hour training the trainers program on "Protective Behaviors for Children" revealing the fact that I had been sexually abused from the ages of 2 through 8 years old; my developmental years.

There were perhaps 30 people in this session, including a counselor from the Rainbow Secondary School which is owned by Jaleh and Mr. Manzidi. (sp?) This was basically a lecture studded with personal experiences and the fact that my healing journey had been supported by the Revelation of Bahá'u'lláh, which had taught me obedience to a spiritual authority as well as teaching me right from wrong, when from my father, I learned immoral behavior.

On Friday, April 13th I returned to Lifeline Botswana where a new group of (35) people had gathered with a few from the previous program.

One young woman, Joyce[22], unknowingly led me into a personal interview of my life for 45 minutes which created depth to the planned workshop. This was no longer a "lecture". I purposely reviewed what I had taught the day before (for the new people), but ended with a workshop format, having some take the role of workshop leaders and

---

[22] Joyce or Joise brought my program to an oasis in the Kalahari Desert

others the role of children, so they could get the feel of leading children.

Then on Saturday, April 14th, I presented "Empowering Our Daughters", to another group of perhaps 35 people, to show them a comparison between the passive, disempowered daughter and young girls who are supported and raised to be heroes, finishing with two stories from my book "The Heroic Female Spirit" – "The Girl Who Climbed a Ladder to the Stars", and "The Legend of the Guardians of the Forest", which illustrate the heroic girl.

Lifeline Botswana will carry on these programs in my absence with the purpose of spreading them to every child 9 years old and under throughout the entire country of Botswana. I believe starting in Francistown, Botswana.

(I also performed as a storyteller at two dinners Friday and Saturday evenings. Children, youth and adults were all attentive and loved the stories with the youth praising them highly.)

On Sunday, Lolly (a former member of the Continental Board of Counselors) and her husband, Gerald Warren, arrived from Lebotse (45 minutes from Gaborone). I was able to introduce my programs sufficiently to Lolly that she, in turn, wants to introduce them into the schools of Lebotse.

On Monday, April 16th, I gave a Fireside to approximately 28 older youth and adults at Rosa and Borzud's home in Block 9 of Gaborone. It was an effort to teach about the equality of women. I could sense the frustration of the men as they told about how the women were using their "freedom" to go to bars to drink, and to smoke.

On Tuesday, April 17th, I departed from Botswana and flew to Johannesburg, arriving at 12:30 PM. Bob Van der Wege (Sherri), formerly from my hometown, Rockford, Illinois, now living in Johannesburg, picked me up, took me to their apartment for lunch, and for an SAfm Radio Station taped interview with _____ to be broadcast at a later time. From there, we picked up Sherri and went to the Bahá'í National Center where I gave a 2 hour workshop on "Protective Behaviors for Children". There are two people there who want to spread my program in Johannesburg. There was a 14 year old girl from Alexandra to whom I gave a copy of my book, "The Heroic Female Spirit"…writing inside the cover, "May God guide and prepare you to become a heroic leader of women"

Bob had driven me through Alexandra, the shanty town that is still impoverished by racism/apartheid. A mother and her 14 year old daughter from Alexandra attended my workshop. I gave the young girl a copy of my book, "The Heroic Female Spirit."

Everywhere I went I gave my business card with my website on it and told them that my programs are free to download. I also gave $100 to Bob Van der Wege to print copies of my programs for those who do not have access to a computer.

I gave a piece of the House of Worship from the reconstruction that was lovingly given to me by Kim Babb, to Lolly and Gerald Warren, and to the Secretary of the National Spiritual Assembly of South Africa. They will place them in an appropriate receptacle for viewing and sharing with other believers.

Follow up E-Mails

Present correspondence includes my e-mail

to_____

Dear _____,

Please be sure to tell your counselors to visit my website where I have new additions. All three of my videos can be viewed for free at my website. They are about abuse issues and taking responsibility for our healing as adults.......sharing feelings.....and expressing anger in appropriate ways.

Also, please inform me of your plans to spread "Protective Behaviors for Children" throughout Botswana. Will you send it to different NGO's that you have e-mail addresses in your computer? Are some of the attendees of the conference we held from different parts of Botswana? I think I heard you mention something about starting in Francistown. Is that correct?

Please let me know of your progress or of any way I can help from this distance. Gentle thoughts, Phyllis

Hey Phyllis

Hope you are well. Thanks for your email. Yes, we have been having trouble with our internet but its now ok.

I will let the participants know of the additions to your website and some of the participants were from different NGOs. Yes we are busy trying to set up centers in Francistown and Maun and hopefully we can reach more people out there. We are also planning to spread your programme, it was very beneficial having you come to present it to us. We were honored and have a lot of respect and admiration for you. The ball is now on our court and we shall inform you of every step we take towards achieving our desired goal.

Thanks once again.

Love, _____,

(The Ministry of Social Services for the Government of Botswana did, indeed, spread the program all over the country to children 9 years old and younger over a period of 3 years.)

Faux Pas

Whenever I travel to a foreign country, especially when I am among Persians, I invariably commit a faux pas. I was invited to a dinner in my honor at the home of an Iraqi Bahá'í. In my excitement, when I learned that there was to be a party the following night, I assumed that one was also for me. (Hmmmmm.....)

So I was going from person to person inviting everyone to my party, telling them I hoped they could make it. Then I noticed my hostess, (Meena Sabet) back tracking through the crowd correcting my misunderstanding and I realized that I had made a faux pas....the party the next night was for the FAMILY!

In the car on the way home, I told Amin and Meena of my embarrassment...and Amin said, "Don't worry, the worst that could happen is that your invitation would be cancelled." I smiled at his joke.

When I went to bed, I awoke with an anxiety attack at 2 AM worrying about my behavior. After breakfast, I sat with Meena and Thato, and Meena asked me, "How did you sleep last night?"

I replied, "Terrible, I had an anxiety attack at 2 AM.

"Why???"" she inquired. "Because of my faux pas last night!"

"Which one?" She asked!

"Which one??????" Then we died laughing.

.

PART SIX

Marshall Islands

February 6th through the 23rd, 2009

I landed in Majuro, the capital city of the Marshall Islands, on Saturday, February 6th, 2009 and was picked up by Irene Taafaki, the Secretary of the National Spiritual Assembly. She dropped me off at the home of Francis and Agnes Reimers

My contact person for all of my appointments was Borja Milne-Stephen (which is a phonetic spelling), a woman approximately 40 years of age, and very capable. I was handicapped in that I did not have a cell phone that works out of the country, but Borja always managed to get messages to me through Irene.

My first appointment was with an NGO named WUTMI, Women United Together in the Marshall Islands[23].

_____, quite young American ladies and I believe inexperienced, were at once encouraging, discouraging and exclusive rather than inclusive. They said

---

[23] Women United Together Marshall Islands (WUTMI) has been the leading voice breaking the silence on violence against women in the Republic of the Marshall Islands (RMI).

they were willing to have a conference at the ICC, which I believe stands for International Conference Center.

They also wanted me to leave my teaching manual with all of my programs with them for 24 hours. I was unwilling to do so, but managed to get them a flash drive so they could review the programs. I waited for confirmation from them for February 19th, while Borja expanded my itinerary. WUTMI suggested that I contact Youth to Youth, an NGO which has a broad application for everything from health and pregnancy to various types of counseling.

Majuro, the capital, had a Pandanas (Screw Pine - a type of fruit) Festival during which I sat in an outdoor covered market as people passed by. I saw many opportunities to engage passersby. I introduced myself as a member of the Bahá'í Faith and my purpose of presenting "Protective Behaviors for Children" to Elder Hicks of the Church of Jesus Christ Latter Day Saints, and his wife, inviting them to attend the conference at the ICC. They were sincerely interested. Two nuns passed by and I told them of the conference as well, introducing myself as a Bahá'í. Following that the President of the Majuro Stake of the Church of Jesus Christ Latter Day Saints passed by with his wife. I introduced myself as a Bahá'í and invited them to attend the conference at ICC. I told them that I served on the board of the Rockford Interfaith Council and had conducted a three part program with their church, the Bahá'ís and the Muslim Community Center on "The Power of Purity" for youth two years ago. They also seemed genuinely interested and told me that 50% of the population of the Marshall Islands was 13 years old and under which indicated that there were children having children. The population for the Marshall Islands is approximately 55,000.

I spoke to two Baptist Missionaries, Rev. and Mrs. Utter, about the program as well. I was hoping to have an Interfaith representation at the conference. And I truly believed that Bahá'u'lláh had put these specific people in my path.

The following week I gave a two hour presentation to Anne Schuster Qoronalau, who is a professor from the Fiji Islands[24] teaching an early childhood education class at the University of the South Pacific, where Irene Taafaki is the Director. This class consisted of 7 to 9 people. Later that

---

[24] Protective Behaviors for Children has spread to the Fiji Islands and to Malaysia (through a Harvard Student who participated in my program in Beijing, China.

week Irene gathered a few staff members for another presentation of "Protective Behaviors for Children." We, also, as the main purpose, brainstormed regarding a booklet the National Spiritual Assembly wants to produce that would focus on how to rear children in families that are violence free, what they would consist of, what kind of support parents and children would need, for distribution in the Marshall Islands. It is a task that was requested by the National Spiritual Assembly. This would be a vital follow-up for the UN Day for the Elimination of Violence Against Women that was held successfully on November 22, 2008.

The next week Borja and I went to visit Youth to Youth and spoke with their Counselor, Camilla Ingram, a woman approximately 55 years old. She had her youth representative, Thata, upload my programs from my flash drive. I presented Camilla with a hard copy of my Chastity and Abstinence workshop for future use. Camilla was a very receptive person and we talked with her for about an hour. She said she was highly interested in the Protective Behaviors for Children presentation and that she would send Thata as a representative to the conference at ICC.

Camilla and I talked woman to woman about crises that we had faced, and supported one another during our conversation. It was a good meeting. Irene later informed me that many of the Baha'i youth in the community drop away from the Faith because they cannot reconcile their lives to Baha'u'llah's Laws on chastity and marriage. Camilla was interested in my program.

I met _____ from WUTMI by accident while shopping and she invited me upstairs to their office. I informed _____ regarding all the people I was fortunate to have met and invited to the program. I gave her a listing of the people to call because they had changed the conference from ICC to the WUTMI office, which I thought was strange. Finally, they changed the date of the conference to February 18th. I also asked if they were going to print my handouts for the presentation. They said they had toner problems. So I printed 35 copies of all of my handouts.

Borja and I arrived at the WUTMI meeting at 9 AM on February 18th and were informed that ONLY staff would attend; that they had tried to call the people I had invited but there was no answer; and then _____ said to _____ "Lock the doors!" Meanwhile, I am trying to puzzle out this strange behavior while at the same time ready my mind for the 3 hour workshop. The two Americans had changed their story about three times and I felt that power had been taken from me, but perhaps they thought I was trying to take power away from them because the contacts had come so swiftly to me. It was a disappointment, but I had to let it go!

Borjia contacted me and let me know that the Ministry of Internal Affairs for the Marshall Islands wanted me to present to a group of 12 to 15 counselors who were available on February 19th. The Ministry of Internal Affairs governs the Adoption Department, all the Mayors of the tiny villages on the outer islands and the Radio Station. I was to find out after my presentation that a representative of the Adoption Department, a police detective and Thata from Youth to Youth were among those who were present at that event. The program was held at the International Women's Teaching Center which is close to the University of the South Pacific campus. The women explained to me that there would have been more counselors there, but they were engaged at another conference running simultaneous to mine.

There was a lot of dialog and questions after my program, which revealed to me both the needs of the culture as well as the need for education. For example, one woman asked me if an ancient story was true that when a girl and boy who were sister and brother had intercourse and conceived, it would result in the birth of an animal. We all assured her that that would not be the case, but it might result in a weaker constitution or lesser intelligence for the child. And that the purpose of the origination of that particular story in their culture may have been a warning.

She also wondered if the instructions in my program would really work in their culture. I assured her that they would work and that they had the power to change their culture. I asked her to visualize one child from nine through three years of age being able to understand, then five or more, and whether it was worth it to try for those children. Then, further to imagine all the counselors in the Marshall Islands working for the same goal.

I then told them the story of how a Bahá'í attorney had come to the help of a woman who was imprisoned in the United States because she had to flee her country, Togo, or endure Female Genital Mutilation. Because of constant negative media attention, the Imam/Chief of the tribe, who was used to being held in high regard, lost respect in the face of the world and who then decided to teach against the practice of FGM. This is an example of education changing the culture in which we live. And if such a horrendous practice could be stopped, so could incestuous behavior.

The president of the Church of Jesus Christ Latter Day Saints Stake of Majuro told me that syphilis is rising rapidly and my research before I flew there indicated that the Marshall Islands are poised for an epidemic of HIV/AIDS. Although HIV/AIDS infection rates are currently low, the Pacific Islands have all the necessary ingredients for a serious epidemic: Poverty, illiteracy, sexual exploitation of children, and the prevalence of unsafe sexual practices (such as multiple partners and a reluctance to use condoms) and the fact that the numbers of sex workers are increasing. The numbers of suicide in the Marshall Islands are the highest in the world. The foregoing information is from a UNICEF Report on line.

My belief is that a major effort to combat incest would go a long way towards not only protecting the children, which are the future of the Marshall Islands, but that teaching the spiritual underpinnings of chastity is vital and vital NOW! This would do a lot toward stemming the tide of HIV/AIDS.

My research before I went to Swaziland and Botswana, countries known for people seeking multiple partners, turned up the fact that Uganda and Thailand, known to have high rates of multiple partners, are two countries that successfully dropped to a lower percentage rate of HIV/AIDS. In Uganda the government brought in international NGO's to teach the local NGO's. The local NGOs taught at the grass roots level.

It became part of the social communication instead of a taboo subject. As a result,
59% of the population decided to have one partner only, called "zero grazing", and 29% chose abstinence. My goal is seeking out those who would choose chastity and abstinence. I believe they are there, waiting.

My purpose in teaching Protective Behaviors for Children is to educate both parents, especially the mother, and the child, to give them tools to become aware of sexual boundaries. I was told that after this program, "word of mouth" began to spread in a very exciting way. And that the Ministry of Internal Affairs had designs to bring me back to the Marshall Islands to present a more expansive conference, and wanted me to design a special conference for men only.

While I was there I participated in three devotionals and was asked to do some storytelling. I also did two Firesides, one was one hour long with the son of my host and hostess. When Francis and Agnes returned from the outer island, they brought back a report of 9 declarations, which could have been more but they ran out of declaration cards. They have rectified this situation. Francis was able to tell one of my stories (about criticism) to the group on the outer island.

I also taught my hostess how to make Lasagna in brutal heat and humidity.

PART SEVEN
Johannesburg and
KwaZulu-Natal
April 6th – April 27th, 2013

April 6th: Traveled from Chicago to Amsterdam to Johannesburg.

April 7th: Arrival in Johannesburg on Sunday. Met by Massoud Derakhshani and Johnson Attah Baaffour. We drove to Massoud's home in Laura's Place, a gated community with a brick wall and a 9 tiered electric fence above.

April 8th: Rested. Mojgan Derkhshani's sister, Mahnaz, and her husband Dr. Nassir Khayyam arrived. Mahnaz has breast cancer and has come to Johannesburg for radiation treatment. I had originally met them during my trip to Swaziland in September of 2006. John and I slept off our jet lag.

April 9th: Nothing planned. More rest, then a Feast.

April 10th: Visited the National Bahá'í Center and met with Kully, the Secretary of the NSA. Purchased some prayer books at the Book store.

April 11th: We went to a Fireside on Science and Religion that was given by Mr. Rowhani. My husband, John Peterson, who is not a Bahá'í was very impressed.

April 12th: Went to Thandspruit, a place that Massoud says is the 2nd most dangerous place in Johannesburg to teach 15 young girls and two boys, ages 13 to 15 years old. I told stories about women and girls as heroes. I was asked to not teach about Protective Behaviors for Children as some of the children were being abused. That evening I taught three neighborhood boys at Mojgan and Massoud's house on the patio.

Saturday, April 13th: Flew to Richards Bay in KwaZulu-Natal Province. Arrived at 10:00 AM. Waited till 2 PM for Johnson, my contact who arranged my itinerary, and Koffi and Sharon, his friends, to pick us up. We did not know that Johnson's car was still not working and that Koffi had two flat tires that had to be fixed and that was the reason they were so late to pick us up. We went to the Boardwalk Mall for lunch, where I gave a program on abuse issues for 3 young ladies and one young man, who are studying at the university, tying it in with how my programs are inspired by the Writings of Bahá'u'lláh. The young man's name means "Challenge." After that group I taught one 23 year old woman and one 19 year old young man. At first they seemed uninterested but as I went along they became very attentive, asking questions that were thought provoking. That night, after a 2 ½ hour drive we arrived at Jozini River Lodge where I was to stay for the next two weeks.

Sunday, April 14th: Breakfast at the lodge and a visit to the grocery store to stock up on a 5 liter bottle of clean water, snacks, travel alarm and more. Today we were to meet the Induna, (Tribal Chief), of Mseleni, but because of a death in the family, the meeting was canceled.

Monday, April 15th: My husband, John, left for Richards Bay for a return trip to Johannesburg. He was kindly driven by Koffi, Johnson's friend, leaving at 4 AM, taking time off from work to do so.

At 8 AM Johnson and I arrived at the Igugulesizwe High School where I was introduced at the morning assembly to all the students. All throughout the day Johnson and I were assisted by Mr. Mjadu Armstrong who streamlined my classes so that I could teach all grades easily. I taught "Protective Behaviors for Children", "Boundaries for Youth", and remaining faithful to one partner. These topics are essential in the Province of KwaZulu-Natal where the percentage of HIV/AIDS infection rate is 42%. Plus, they have a high rate of child sexual abuse. It is "normal" in the Zulu nation for a man to grab a woman's breast or buttocks in passing. At the end of my day, the Zulu teens performed Zulu dancing and song for me. The harmony was incredible and the youth hooted and hollered and screamed when I got up to dance with them. Even when the Zulu children and youth speak, it sounds as if they are singing. I fell in love with this school.

Monday night at 7 Johnson and I met the Ghanaian Community of Jozini. Koffi and his wife welcomed me into their home as though I was family. I shared with them what I was teaching in the schools and told stories of women and girls as heroes, based on my book "The Heroic Female Spirit." I also shared the song that is based on

"Protective Behaviors for Children" and they were delighted with it, including their First Grade Daughter, Sisi, who now teaches it to other children in the neighborhood.

Tuesday, April 16th: I continued my workshops at Igugulesizwe High School at 8 AM through 3 PM, with a one hour break. I was on my feet 6 hours both days. I wear very sturdy shoes. That evening we had dinner with the Principal of the school and I presented copies of my books to him, telling him there was a curriculum within each book. I asked him how to spell his name to be polite and he said "My name is William Shakespeare." And he left it at that. I will get it from Johnson before I send this report. He begged me to come back within 6 months. I told him I would try to do that. The need is so great.

Wednesday, April 17th: Today At 8 AM I was introduced to Ms. Lukhele, a Life Skills Educator at the Siqakatha Primary School. I made a presentation of my books and CD to her. As I taught the Fourth, Fifth and Sixth Grade Children, I could hear goats who were roaming free on the school grounds crying outside the doors. My program involved "Protective Behaviors for Children," and my CD "Don't be a Bully! Be a Buddy!" The children loved the songs and followed along on the song sheets. Ms. Lukhele drove me back to the Jozini River Lodge and 200 yards from the gate, she told me to look at a man who was walking toward us. I saw a bearded man with long hair who looked disheveled. She then said, "He raped a 14 year old girl in my school." I was thankful that she identified him to me. And I was also thankful that the Lodge had a gate on it. I made a commitment to Ms. Lukhele that I would send markers for the children in her school.

Thursday, April 18th: The school that I taught at today was a Primary Catholic Boarding School. I made a presentation of my books and CD. Prior to my visit it was discovered that 26 children had been sexually abused and physically beaten by the Boarding Master, who told them he would kill them if they told. Unfortunately, the Sisters of the School believed the Boarding Master instead of the children. This happens often. As I presented the "Protective Behaviors Program", I saw the Sisters in the back of the hall and wondered what they were thinking. The students were very attentive to the program and they loved the "Private Place Song" that I taught them.

_____ 12 year old son was a student at this school and was severely beaten. She saw the bruises and was shocked and begged him to tell her what was happening. She assisted in the presentation of the program and became a Bahá'í after I left South Africa. The Principal, _____, who had a death in the family, was supposed to go to a different workshop on this day; he chose to stay and watch my workshop instead. After he saw the positive reaction of the children and the Sisters, he said, "I want to use my school as a nucleus for spreading this "Protective Behaviors for Children Program" throughout the Province of KwaZulu-Natal." At that point I started crying. Sister Hildegard grabbed me and hugged me and told me that the program was wonderful. I could tell that the staff at the Catholic Boarding School had really been suffering.

That evening Johnson, Sharon, and I met with the Nongoma Branch of the Rotary Club. Teachers of the Boarding school attended this informal meeting and one Doctor who was present was impressed that I encouraged the children to follow Jesus rather than take this opportunity to teach about the Baha'i Faith. After all, I believe my early spiritual education in the Baptist Church led me to Bahá'u'lláh.

Friday, April 19th: Visited the Jozini Municipality Library to use the computer to e-mail my husband and my Bahá'í Community at home.

Saturday, April 20th: Conducted a "Protective Behaviors For Children Workshop" at the Mseleni Children's Home, run by Ms. Fredlund. There were children here in ill fitting clothes and without shoes. They were very responsive to the program.

Sunday, April 21st: Today there were 20 church members and a few Ghanaian friends who gathered at Mr. and Mrs. Buthelezi's home as I presented storytelling about Heroes and Heroines, the Traumatized Soul, Abuse, and the purpose of my visit. The group decided to form a committee after we conducted an open forum. It is the wish of the group that I return and conduct workshops for ADULTS on the following:

1: Protective Behaviors for Children
2: The Importance of the Development of a Feeling Language for Children and Adults.
3: Anger Alternatives

4: Authority of Self

5: Remaining Faithful to your Spouse

6: Boundaries for Youth and Adults

7: Parenting

There was a Zulu woman present who was the head of an NGO for women who was highly interested in seeing this come about.

Monday, April 22nd: We left the Jozini River Lodge at 6:15 AM for the Mavela High School. Assembly was at 8 AM, then I taught "Protective Behaviors to grades 8 and 9, followed by the Boundary Game and a talk on HIV/AIDS, plus a talk on Vignettes for discussion and One Sexual Partner, for grades 10 through 12th. After the program, one 10th grade boy yelled out "I will NEVER forget this day." Another teenage boy shouted, "This is the best day of my life!!"

This afternoon Johnson and I went to the Jozini Municipality Library to make a formal presentation of Four of my books, "Assisting the Traumatized Soul," "Healing the Wounded Soul," "The Heroic Female Spirit," and "Remaining Faithful."

And this evening we went to Mkuze to have dinner with Sharon Nkosi and just relax while we chatted.

Tuesday, April 23rd: We left Jozini River Lodge at 6:15 AM for Okhayeni Primary School. Mrs. Nokukhanya Noloyu was the principal.

These children carried their desks and chairs outside to be placed under three large Umbrella Thorn trees in the school yard. I taught "Protective Behaviors for Children" and told a story about anger that were both translated by Mrs. Noloyu. I also taught about "feelings" (especially anger) and was told by one assistant that it went with their life skills program hand in hand. They enjoyed the "Don't be a Bully! Be a Buddy!" songs. These were grades 4, 5, 6, and 7. I told the story of "Randy and Butch Learn to Discharge Anger." I made a presentation of my books and CD to Mrs. Noloyu for their future use.

Wednesday, April 24th: There was a reception planned for me at the Conference Room at the Jozini River Lodge, owned by Dr. Oni, a family practitioner. He was present for the "Good-bye." And quite unexpectedly four Counselors from the Government and from four separate

Municipalities were present. I recapped what I had accomplished in the two weeks I was in KwaZulu-Natal and what I hoped to do in October upon my return if funded by an organization.

Johnson and I do not know how these four counselors found out about the reception; he had tried to get government people involved two months before I arrived in KwaZulu-Natal, but was not successful, so we were very grateful that the hand of God brought them in.

Thursday, April 25th: Johnson arrived at 6:15 AM. I was all packed and we emptied my hotel room. We left the Lodge for Igugulesizwe High School arriving in time for the students to say goodbye during Assembly. The Principal said to me "You have lifted the mood of the entire school with your visit!" One young Poet wrote a poem about my visit and recited it. I hope to get a copy. Then they performed songs and dances again. Following that I gave a presentation to a group of approximately 160 Tertiary University Students from 8 till 9 AM, and then we left to drive to Richards Bay for my flight back to Johannesburg at 1:15 PM.

Friday, April 26th: Back to Johannesburg. This was a day of rest and reunion with Mojgan and Massoud, Mahnaz and Dr. Nasser.

Saturday, April 27th: I boarded my plane to Paris and then to Chicago,.

I was very grateful to be able to have served the Principals, Teachers, Students, Adults and Parents of KwaZulu-Natal. In all I taught 5,000 Students and 4 hundred educators. Inshallah I will return!

I could not have done this without the help of Johnson Attah-Baaffour, who has tremendous marketing skills. Nor could I have accomplished my mission without the assistance of the teachers and the life skills educators who saw the value of the programs. I spent one hour each day in prayer and that carried me through the difficult moments, knowing that my community back home in Rockford was praying for me. Another comfort that I had was the fact that during every travel teaching trip I take, I spend 1 hour studying "Tablets of Bahá'u'lláh.

I also have to acknowledge Mojgan Derkhshani's participation in this adventure. If she hadn't sent me a Facebook Birthday greeting on October 11th, 2012 with an invitation to visit her in Johannesburg, I would not have realized this opportunity. Her social grace led me to inquire with the National Spiritual Assembly of South Africa and I am deeply grateful to Mojgan and Kully, the secretary of the NSA of South Africa.

67590580R00139

Made in the USA
Lexington, KY
17 September 2017